American Politics: A Very Short Introduction

VERY SHORT INTRODUCTIONS are for anyone wanting a stimulating and accessible way in to a new subject. They are written by experts and have been published in more than 25 languages worldwide.

The series began in 1995 and now represents a wide variety of topics in history, philosophy, religion, science, and the humanities. The VSI library now contains more than 300 volumes—a Very Short Introduction to everything from ancient Egypt and Indian philosophy to conceptual art and cosmology—and will continue to grow in a variety of disciplines.

Very Short Introductions available now:

ADVERTISING Winston Fletcher
AFRICAN HISTORY John Parker and
    Richard Rathbone
AGNOSTICISM Robin Le Poidevin
AMERICAN HISTORY Paul S. Boyer
AMERICAN IMMIGRATION
    David A. Gerber
AMERICAN POLITICAL PARTIES
    AND ELECTIONS L. Sandy Maisel
THE AMERICAN PRESIDENCY
    Charles O. Jones
ANAESTHESIA Aidan O'Donnell
ANARCHISM Colin Ward
ANCIENT EGYPT Ian Shaw
ANCIENT GREECE Paul Cartledge
ANCIENT PHILOSOPHY Julia Annas
ANCIENT WARFARE Harry Sidebottom
ANGELS David Albert Jones
ANGLICANISM Mark Chapman
THE ANGLO-SAXON AGE John Blair
THE ANIMAL KINGDOM
    Peter Holland
ANIMAL RIGHTS David DeGrazia
THE ANTARCTIC Klaus Dodds
ANTISEMITISM Steven Beller
ANXIETY Daniel Freeman
    and Jason Freeman
THE APOCRYPHAL GOSPELS
    Paul Foster
ARCHAEOLOGY Paul Bahn
ARCHITECTURE Andrew Ballantyne
ARISTOCRACY William Doyle
ARISTOTLE Jonathan Barnes

ART HISTORY Dana Arnold
ART THEORY Cynthia Freeland
ATHEISM Julian Baggini
AUGUSTINE Henry Chadwick
AUSTRALIA Kenneth Morgan
AUTISM Uta Frith
THE AZTECS David Carrasco
BARTHES Jonathan Culler
BEAUTY Roger Scruton
BESTSELLERS John Sutherland
THE BIBLE John Riches
BIBLICAL ARCHAEOLOGY Eric H. Cline
BIOGRAPHY Hermione Lee
THE BLUES Elijah Wald
THE BOOK OF MORMON
    Terryl Givens
BORDERS Alexander C. Diener and
    Joshua Hagen
THE BRAIN Michael O'Shea
BRITISH POLITICS Anthony Wright
BUDDHA Michael Carrithers
BUDDHISM Damien Keown
BUDDHIST ETHICS Damien Keown
CANCER Nicholas James
CAPITALISM James Fulcher
CATHOLICISM Gerald O'Collins
THE CELL Terence Allen and
    Graham Cowling
THE CELTS Barry Cunliffe
CHAOS Leonard Smith
CHILDREN'S LITERATURE
    Kimberley Reynolds
CHINESE LITERATURE Sabina Knight

Available soon:

For more information visit our web site

www.oup.co.uk/general/vsi/

Richard M. Valelly

AMERICAN POLITICS

A Very Short Introduction

OXFORD
UNIVERSITY PRESS

OXFORD
UNIVERSITY PRESS

Oxford University Press is a department of the University of Oxford.
It furthers the University's objective of excellence in research,
scholarship, and education by publishing worldwide.

Oxford   New York
Auckland   Cape Town Dar es Salaam   Hong Kong   Karachi
Kuala Lumpur   Madrid   Melbourne   Mexico City   Nairobi
New Delhi   Shanghai   Taipei   Toronto

With offices in
Argentina   Austria   Brazil   Chile   Czech Republic   France   Greece
Guatemala   Hungary   Italy   Japan   Poland   Portugal   Singapore
South Korea   Switzerland   Thailand   Turkey   Ukraine   Vietnam

Oxford is a registered trademark of Oxford University Press
in the UK and certain other countries.

Published in the United States of America by
Oxford University Press
198 Madison Avenue, New York, NY 10016

Library of Congress Cataloging-in-Publication Data
Valelly, Richard M.
American politics : a very short introduction / Richard M. Valelly.
p.   cm.—(Very short introductions)
Includes bibliographical references and index.
ISBN 978-0-19-537385-1 (pbk. : alk. paper)
1. United States—Politics and government. I. Title.
JK275.V36   2013
320.473—dc23   2012024527

1 3 5 7 9 8 6 4 2

Printed in Great Britain
by Ashford Colour Press Ltd., Gosport, Hants.
on acid-free paper

For Americanists everywhere

Contents

List of illustrations

Acknowledgments

Nick Allred, Swarthmore College '13, did fact-checking, assembled the references and the art list, and wrote the first drafts of the captions for the figures as I finalized the manuscript. Sonia Tycko of Oxford University Press efficiently and calmly handled dozens of last-minute details and requests and provided valuable editorial tips. Nancy Toff of Oxford University Press was a tough and effective editor who greatly improved the manuscript. Kathryn Hodson, Special Collections Department Manager, University of Iowa Libraries, helped with use of the image for figure 7, and Bill Alkofer of Minneapolis, Minnesota, graciously provided the image for figure 9. Martha Derthick, Chris Howard, Rich Kazis, Suzanne Mettler, Gigi Simeone, Nanette Tobin, and Ben Yagoda gave me invaluable comments on chapter drafts. Some years ago Sandy Maisel helped me to understand what I was getting myself into in writing a VSI. Any and all mistakes in this book are my responsibility alone.

Chapter 1
Elements of American democracy

American politics presents a carnival of quarrels, featuring the two political parties, interest groups, political movements, and often protest in the streets. Sign-waving opponents greet the president of the United States wherever he travels. But American politics also offers—more than citizens and pundits recognize—scenes of legislative deliberation and agreement between the country's contentious political parties.

Judges come into this public sphere too. Politicians and groups invite or petition the Supreme Court to adjudicate policy disputes in ways that they prefer. Yet the justices decide their cases according to legal reasoning and their own political values. The results simultaneously frustrate and satisfy the president, Congress, the political parties, advocacy groups, and individual citizens. American politics thus combines conflict and cooperation, partisanship and contests over public law.

Less likely to attract the notice of citizens but equally important in the political arena are national regulatory agencies. They carry on vital work amid the interbranch disagreements about policy and constitutional meaning. These include the Federal Reserve (the nation's central bank) and the Environmental Protection Agency.

No mention of such agencies can be found in the Constitution of 1787; Congress did not create them via constitutional amendment, but Congress legislated them into existence. These more modern institutions compose an administrative state.

The Constitution also presupposes the existence of subnational governments—that is, the states—from Alabama to Wyoming. Each has separation of powers constitutions and bills of rights of their own. The states legally charter local governments, particularly school boards, counties, cities, and municipalities, and special governments (such as authorities for managing the use of land or water resources). The local governments for their part have developed such important institutions as police and fire departments, public transportation authorities, zoning boards, and tax assessment commissions.

In all, the United States has a very large number of political and governmental players who are constantly busy with politicking, judging, and administering. What connects them to the wishes of citizens? Those who clock in every day at America's public institutions do so with the approval of many if not most of their fellow citizens. To get that approval they have stood for office in elections—or the people who have appointed them have stood for office. Many try to keep their pulse on public opinion, and they monitor what the media and other critics of their performance are saying about them.

The quest for public support invites extra-constitutional players to publicize or to influence the activities of officeholders and the procedures of national, state, and local governments. They include political reporters and editorial page writers at newspapers or online publications; politically connected law firms, which raise money according to campaign finance law; voluntary associations, such as trade unions, which make phone calls on behalf of candidate or good government groups that endorse candidates, and preachers at churches who tell their flocks whom to vote for.

Some citizens, working through social movements, pour time and energy into politics by marching, picketing, postering, blogging, and the like. A modest percentage of the public also contacts public officials. These citizens write letters, call Capitol Hill, or send emails. They do so in reaction to public events and crises, or they do so because interest groups and party organizations have asked them to.

A highly active set of Americans interact professionally with public officials in state capitals and Washington, D.C. Many of these lobbyists are well tailored and highly paid. In Hollywood, Houston, or Manhattan, among other places, rich and glamorous people attend fund-raisers for professional politicians or well-financed advocacy groups. But surprisingly, many so-called lobbyists are also advocates for citizen groups or trade unions.

The most consequential extra-constitutional institutions are the networks of organizations connected to the two major political parties, Democrats and Republicans. Webs of formal fund-raising organizations, legislative caucuses, consulting firms, and opinion research firms are associated with them. These two parties are, in fact, essential orchestrators of the processes by which office-seekers try to gain popular approval. Modern democracy is inconceivable without competitive political parties. Parties create, first, a vital vocation. They do that because they alone legitimately install people in public office. The Chamber of Commerce cannot elect a senator or president, for example.

Parties provide the prospect of decently compensated work as professional representatives. For the more talented politicians, political parties provide career ladders. Through affiliating with a political party a state representative or senator might aspire to be a member of Congress—and from there move (as Abraham Lincoln or Barack Obama did) to the White House. Party politicians as a class are not particularly well liked, but most of them are skillful professionals. Their work typically involves both personal sacrifices and an ethically informed ability to balance means and ends while seeking and holding public office.

Besides providing cadres of representatives, political parties in the United States also offer distinct policy programs to the public—indeed, they offer elaborate and rival views of what the purposes of government are. By talking to voters about civic ideals and public policy, professional politicians perform another essential service: they *attach* otherwise busy and distracted citizens *to* public affairs. Political parties, over and over, according to the required electoral schedule of the Constitution and the state provisions, gather and focus the attention of citizens. They also mold their political identities. Through voting in many elections over the course of their adult lives, through paying attention to news and advertisements during campaigns, and by tuning in to the public debates after elections about what the results meant, citizens acquire political identities. They become "liberal Democrats," for instance, or "conservative Republicans." Party politics is indeed broadly educative.

Democratic politics, in short, demands effort. What makes people do it? Many politicians, activists, and citizens find political activity exhilarating. They worry less than others about giving up privacy, spare time, or higher income in the private sector for whatever mark they might be lucky enough to make through public office or political activity. Politics, it seems, is its own reward.

But most Americans in and out of public office also have extrinsic and specific goals that motivate them. Party politicians will want a simpler tax code, say, or want to do something about global warming. Citizens and groups, for their part, also try to get things from government: either private goods, such as tax breaks, or some bigger, more public good, such as a solution for the lack of health insurance among a growing number of Americans. They try to stop government from doing things, such as the antiwar movement during the Vietnam era. They try to stop government

4

from becoming too large. After all, there is a strongly libertarian, antigovernment streak in American political life. Or a group will try to place an item on the agenda of public discussion—say income inequality, dramatized by the phrase, "we are the 99 percent."

But besides having goals or issue preferences, people in politics also reflect and comment on how well the political system works. Citizens and politicians alike know that some political practices are essential for the proper functioning of liberal democracy.

There are many such practices, and there are disagreements about their relative importance. Most observers of democracy, though, value good public deliberation: argumentation from rival points of view. In the United States the separation of powers and political party competition for voter approval promote that principle. Congress and the president discuss policy; Democrats and Republicans do the same. They discuss policy and issues all the time—quietly and informally in cloakrooms, on Sunday morning talk shows, by giving rival press conferences, through campaign debate appearances, through meetings with editorial boards, through the give-and-take of committee hearings. Often the talk is harsh in tone. But public deliberation is vigorous enough for much of American democracy to resemble government-by-discussion.

There is a second principle or criterion: that the majority should rule. American politics is famous for the protections it provides to territorially located minorities—in the U.S. Senate, for instance, which places the population of North Dakota on an equal footing with the population of California in legislative deliberation. Likewise the Electoral College seems to give Idaho, North Dakota, South Dakota, and Wyoming voters much more weight than those in California, Florida, New York, or Texas.

But many majoritarian features are woven into the fabric of American politics through the office-seeking activities of party politicians. The House of Representatives is elected by popular majorities, and almost always the president gains office through winning a popular majority. Senators may represent small states, but they also represent popular majorities in those states. Majority rule is valuable because it confers legitimacy on what officials do.

A third significant benchmark for assessing any democracy is that of governmental competence. Whether government actually *is* competent is fiercely debated, and many people believe that it can never be especially competent. But if one admits that government can at least *sometimes* be relatively competent, able to perform a task or to stop performing it when told to, then one can see that there are connections among governmental competence, political discussion, and majority choice. Both discussion of what to do about a public issue (and of course majority rule) would mean little if democratic government is unable to do what people call upon it to do.

At the same time, public discussion, including the complaining about government that is endemic in American public life, probably enhances governmental competence. Policy ideas and government actions must survive public debate on their merits. Public debate helps Congress, the president, and the people who work in the executive branch to figure out whether they are doing a good job. It is by no means a sufficient source of information on whether they are leading, legislating, and governing well. But it is quite necessary.

A fourth criterion for assessing a democracy is its freedom of association—that is, the liberty to gather in meetings or to formally join an association without threat from either the government or frightened, angry mobs. Where does that liberty come from in the United States? One can find it in the Constitution, particularly in the First Amendment (which protects "the right of the people peaceably to assemble"). The Supreme Court and civil liberties lawyers did much to strengthen the First Amendment during the twentieth century. But party conflict and competition reinforce associational rights, for party competition intrinsically promotes freedom of association and speech. Parties hold meetings, rallies, and conventions, after all, and their conventions invite protesters. They and their supporters buy airtime for issue ads and for candidate advocacy and critique.

Government activity by itself invites citizens to band together. Congressional consideration of policy issues and the development of federal agencies stimulates the formation of associations to influence congressional deliberation and monitor bureaucratic behavior. Lobbying is a pejorative term for that activity, but lobbying itself ought to be seen as one vital facet of the freedom of association. The National Association of Manufacturers lobbies Congress, but so does the Friends Committee on National Legislation, a Quaker organization.

A fifth democratic benchmark is that of accountability. In a representative democracy, representatives must give an account of what they do or have done with their office. They may try to mislead those to whom they are accountable. But the party-managed processes of competition for office inhibit the abuse of accountability. Parties have platforms and stances that sharply simplify how officeholders explain themselves to voters. Parties also field rivals to incumbents or rival aspirants to office if an incumbent retires. If one side stretches the truth, the other side is there to point that out.

Gaps in representation

A sixth criterion is the equal representation of everyone's political preferences. Equal representation of everyone is the least satisfied standard, however, not only in America but also in all democracies. This is because democratic government-by-discussion requires both an agenda of items to debate *and* equal distribution of resources to set that agenda. The distribution of agenda-setting resources is, however, unequal and uneven.

New items come onto the agenda of national debate because politicians hunt for novel issues to help their careers or their political parties. Party politicians respond to new demands by groups with which they are already allied. They respond to sustained protest, and to crises and events such as 9/11, economic downturns, or fierce hurricanes that knock out whole cities— which, in the case of Hurricane Katrina's 2005 devastation of New Orleans, all too briefly put African American economic and political disadvantage on the national agenda.

But despite the incentives that U.S. politicians have to put new issues on the national agenda and despite the formal freedom to form advocacy groups, glaring gaps in representation have long shadowed the American polity. Racial hierarchy has produced the best known failure. In southern states, efforts by black citizens to form their own advocacy groups and to participate in elections was dangerous for decades after the abolition of slavery. By about 1910 African Americans in the South, where most African Americans resided, found themselves legally barred from voting.

1. Sanitation workers in Memphis, Tennessee, demand workplace justice in 1968. Lacking adequate representation in city government, they turned to strike and protest.

The majority of white Americans therefore ignored segregation and racism during much of the twentieth century. Whites eventually paid attention to segregation and racism—but only because African Americans, through a full decade (1955–65) of courageous, continuous, and nonviolent protest in the South, forced the entire country to debate the racialized limits of American democracy. But that agenda-setting achievement has not been enough. African Americans as a group still struggle with the impact of disenfranchisement and segregation on health, educational attainment, employment, personal wealth, and home ownership.

Today there are other minorities who also need strong representation—disenfranchised ex-felons, Native Americans, the poorly educated, people who have trouble finding regular and rewarding work, lesbians, gays, and other sexual minorities, Latinos, Asian Americans, and Muslims. Their concerns, in a fairer society, would be continuously and fully discussed in public until they were resolved. Similarly, the legal immigrant population would be heard more than it is, to say nothing of the "illegals" who stand in the shadows all around the country.

Such failure to consider the interests of the less powerful may be inevitable in any democracy. That very inevitability means, however, that American democracy is a work in progress. This is the final fundamental feature of American democracy that is worth noting. As Martin Luther King Jr. once wrote, "You cannot depend upon American institutions to function without pressure. Any real change in the status quo depends upon continued creative action to sharpen the conscience of the nation and establish a climate in which even the most recalcitrant elements are forced to admit that change is necessary."

Americans have a vital legacy to protect, and that is the Constitution. By carrying on their struggles with each other in the name of constitutional ideals they do just that—they perpetuate the Constitution. Nevertheless, the public agenda never represents everyone. Public debates are always open to new ways of talking about the concerns of those who need to be heard.

Chapter 2
The presidency

Of all the offices of the United States specified in the Constitution, the presidency is the one that has been most affected by the discipline of political science. America's only PhD political scientist to serve as president, Woodrow Wilson, envisioned an attention-focusing role, one that was not described in the original Constitution. The president, Wilson thought, should be rhetorically adept and should strive to explain public affairs to the citizenry on a regular basis.

Somewhat later in the twentieth century, during the Great Depression, public administration experts helped endow the office of the president with administrative and budgetary expertise—again, layering onto the office responsibilities and roles that the initial Constitution did not specify. Presidents institutionalized and broadened their search for and their use of expert advice and policy information.

The presidency also came to depend on public-opinion research, which is a combination of demography, mathematics, and cognitive psychology. Private national polling operations—some for-profit, such as the Gallup Poll, some not-for-profit, such as the American National Election Studies at the University of Michigan—constantly monitor public opinion and how the public views the president. Presidents themselves directly observe public opinion with their own pollsters.

The rhetorical presidency

The twentieth- and twenty-first-century presidents have constantly spoken to the American public—engaging in town-hall style meetings, giving weekly radio addresses or webcasts, or talking to the country via prime-time speeches. That kind of presidential activity is an informal but profound invention, which can be traced to Woodrow Wilson's impact on the office. It did not come from the rise of new communications technology but came instead from a philosophy of democratic leadership, which over time has strongly shaped the way presidents incorporate communication into the office.

Wilson, while at John Hopkins University, wrote one of the first doctoral dissertations in political science that he later published in 1885 as *Congressional Government: A Study in American Politics*. That book emphasized the centrality of dozens of congressional committees in American national government, operating out of view and with little public accountability. Citizens inevitably needed help in following public affairs. Wilson wanted democratic politics to be *educative*.

When Woodrow Wilson became president, he therefore changed how presidents spoke in public. Theodore Roosevelt, at the onset of the twentieth century, anticipated Wilson's reconceptualization. Roosevelt memorably referred to the office as a "bully pulpit"—by which he did not mean a podium from which to berate others but rather a very good or outstanding soapbox (as in the phrase "what a bully pulpit!") But it was Wilson who saw that he could institutionalize that very phrase.

Summoning an extra session of Congress to Washington to consider cuts in tariffs, Wilson announced that he would deliver the message by opening the session in person. Not since Washington and Adams had a president personally addressed

Congress, but that changed on April 8, 1913, when Wilson briefly addressed a joint session of Congress. Indeed, Wilson personally addressed joint sessions of Congress fifteen times between April 1913 and January 1918—a record that no other president has come close to matching.

2. President Woodrow Wilson personally addresses Congress in 1913 as part of his quest to develop the rhetorical presidency.

Addressing Congress was only part of Wilson's ideal of a rhetorical presidency. In early 1916 Wilson promoted American preparedness in the face of World War I's uncertain and dismaying course. His countrywide tour was an enormous success, cementing Wilson's belief in this sort of communication with the public. The better-known example is his subsequent 1919 tour to explain the Versailles Treaty. He sought to bring the public to his side as he battled a Senate that blocked the treaty. At the height of a circuit that seemed to be replicating his 1916 triumph, Wilson suffered a collapse on his train, and later a near-fatal stroke, effectively ending his presidency and in fact leaving the United States, most ironically, without any presidential government until the election of the ill-starred Warren G. Harding.

Later presidents did not conclude, however, that being explainer-in-chief was bad for their health. When President George W. Bush traveled the nation after his 2004 election to promote the privatization of Social Security, he acted in a perfectly Wilsonian manner—even if he did not have the success that Wilson had in 1916.

One president who dramatically expanded Wilson's rhetorical presidency was Franklin Delano Roosevelt who had served in the Wilson administration as Secretary of the Navy. He communicated with the American public with his "fireside chats" on the radio, as the press dubbed them. (FDR wryly noted that the press insisted on using this term even for those addresses that he gave during crushing summer heat.) Over four consecutive terms in office, Roosevelt gave some thirty-three addresses, all touching on vital public questions, often on Sundays, when citizens had free time to listen to him on their radios. As radio ownership steadily increased, FDR's fireside chats reached more and more citizens.

The emergence and diffusion of television subsequently aided the Wilson-FDR conceptualization of the presidency. In 1950 about 20 percent of American households had black-and-white TVs; by

1960 that number had risen exponentially to 85 percent. And in 1961 John F. Kennedy became the first president to participate in a live television news conference.

Although JFK is indelibly associated with black-and-white TV because of his apparent ease with the medium, his predecessor had in fact shown the way. As television diffused throughout American society, Dwight D. Eisenhower used television in a thoroughly Wilsonian manner, giving a television address on the signing of the Korean armistice (July 26, 1953) and on the Paris NATO conference (December 23, 1957). Eisenhower's farewell address of January 17, 1961, in which he famously warned Americans about the risks to democracy from being on a constant wartime footing, was broadcast on both radio and television.

But with today's 24/7 news shows, dozens of channels, and the rise of online communication, presidents now can hardly connect as dramatically, easily, and unilaterally as they once did. President Obama's first prime-time news conference attracted nearly 50 million viewers. By his fourth such news conference, concerning the exceptionally important topic of his administration's push for a national health care plan, viewership had dropped by half, to about 25 million.

Presidents must work much harder than they once had to in order to get their explanations across. Not only are they trying to influence the print and broadcast media, but they also must contend with a new era of highly decentralized, segmented but nonetheless consequential digital communications: blogs, Twitter, YouTube, and many others. Thus President Obama gave 129 interviews to the press in his first ten months in office— three times the number that his predecessor, George W. Bush, had. As a story in *Time* put it, "The news cycle that once defined the day at the White House has given way to . . . the news cyclone . . . that churns constantly and seems almost impervious to management."

Nowhere is the Wilsonian view of rhetorical leadership described in the original Constitution of 1787. But the presidency has gradually fused with the privately owned and operated communication system comprising print, broadcast, and digital media. Presidents constantly use those communication linkages to talk to the public and to send signals to Capitol Hill.

Seeking advice and information

Franklin D. Roosevelt presided over a proliferation of new authorities, administrations, boards, commissions, corporations, and corps, each with a new acronym—AAA, CCC, FERA, NRA, NLRB, NPB, PWA, RFC, SEC, TVA, WPA—the "alphabet soup" of the New Deal. That helter-skelter administrative expansion raised executive organization and managerial efficiency to top rank on the national agenda, but doing so effectively required expert advice.

Among the efficiency experts who came to the fore was Louis Brownlow, director of the Public Administration Clearing House affiliated with the University of Chicago. Working at breakneck speed in 1933 and 1934, and backed by the recently formed Social Science Research Council, Brownlow participated in a "commission of inquiry" that researched the ways public administration actually worked in the United States. Upon publishing the findings and seeing how widely they were read among the public at large, Brownlow decided that his work had clear implications for "problems in the realm of top management." "That," he later remarked, "led us straight to the White House."

Indeed it did. FDR reached out to Brownlow and company to seek advice on how to better run the executive branch. FDR established the Committee on Administrative Management in March 1936, with Brownlow at its head. Brownlow had worked as a journalist before teaching himself public administration on the job as a District of Columbia commissioner; none other than the professor-become-president Woodrow Wilson had appointed him to that position. Brownlow, along with two leading professors of political science from Chicago and Columbia, quickly fashioned a dramatically and clearly written report, which FDR then submitted to Congress in January 1937. It bluntly stated, "The President needs help" and went on to propose, among other recommendations, the creation of six advisory positions reporting directly to the president "to assist him in obtaining quickly and without delay all pertinent information possessed by any of the executive departments so as to guide him in making his responsible decisions. . . ."

At first, Congress fiercely resisted the Brownlow Committee and its report. The public administration professors proposed the transfer of the then dozen or so independent regulatory commissions (including the Federal Reserve, America's central bank) into the cabinet. They also suggested that the entire country be covered by seven regional agencies akin to the Tennessee Valley Authority, reporting to the president and planning natural resource use. In short they proposed a constitutional revolution.

But FDR and the committee still ended up setting the terms of interbranch deliberation—enough for Congress to produce the Executive Reorganization Act of 1939, creating the Executive Office of the President (EOP). It was a major turning point. Today the EOP handles a very broad policy portfolio. It contains both the White House Office and nine additional units (ranging from the Council of Economic Advisers to the U.S. Trade Representative, or USTR, who is the president's principal trade advisor.) Eight of these units give advice about, as well as directly contribute to the making of, policy. In the White House Office, there are ten units, ranging from the Domestic Policy Council to the Office of the First Lady to the White House Military Office. Of these, seven—such as the Homeland Security Council, led by the Assistant to the President for Homeland Security and Counterterrorism, who serves as the president's homeland security and counterterrorism advisor and who sets the council's meeting agenda—are directly focused on policy and policy advice. President Bill Clinton effected a major addition to this advice-giving environment of the presidency by instituting the National Economic Council—and its director serves "as a coordinator of economic policies and the conduit to the president on domestic and global economic issues."

All of these advice-giving, policy-research, and policy-shaping agencies supplement the cabinet agencies, such as the Department of Agriculture and the Department of the Treasury. But their location inside the presidency itself means that they compete on better terms than the cabinet secretaries for the attention of the president. The Constitution does not tell presidents to seek expert advice and information. But presidents now avail themselves of the permanent and very broad policy-analytic capacities housed within the Executive Office of the President.

Monitoring public opinion

The third way in which political science has shaped the office of president has been through the rise of the public opinion survey and its incorporation into White House analysis of and deliberation over the public mood. Karl Rove, George W. Bush's political consultant, was so central to the Bush administration that Democrats often demonized him as the dark genius of that presidency. Similarly, David Axelrod, candidate Obama's political consultant, became essential to the Obama administration. In 2009, the *New York Times* noted, "There are few words that come across the president's lips that have not been blessed by Mr. Axelrod. He reviews every speech, studies every major policy position. . . ."

The first president to use reliable and representative opinion surveys systematically was FDR, during World War II. FDR sought to ascertain as clearly as he could the public mood at a very dangerous time for the country. He chose to work closely—and secretly—with social psychologist Hadley Cantril of Princeton University. (Cantril, it happened, chose to teach at Princeton because the town in which the university is located was home to one of the founders of opinion research, George Gallup.) As a junior professor, Cantril wrote a pioneering analysis of the mass panic that gripped many CBS radio listeners when Orson Welles broadcast his invasion-from-Mars "War of the Worlds" program on the eve of Halloween, 1938. In his study Cantril identified key personal traits to explain why some citizens panicked when they heard the broadcast while others did not. His work had clear implications for a president weighing how the public mood would help or hinder a transition toward total war. In this instance, the domestic and foreign policy presidencies were deeply intertwined.

The taxpayer never funded FDR's "in-house" polling during WWII—nor has the taxpayer ever paid for any presidential polling. Members of Congress view it suspiciously. Instead, presidential polling is unofficial. It relies on bringing campaign operatives into the White House, and it is paid for by the party of the president (though the staff that analyzes poll results is of course on the public payroll). The precedent that presidential polling is unofficial, informal, and rarely openly discussed was set indeed in the case of Cantril and Roosevelt. A Princeton businessman quietly paid for Cantril's secret analyses for President Roosevelt and for Secretary of State Henry Stimson.

In an assessment that could be applied to the presidents who have used polls extensively—that is, those who have served in the White House since the 1960s—Cantril noted, "President Roosevelt was . . . the most alert responsible official I have ever known to be concerned about public opinion systematically. I never once saw him 'change his mind' because of what any survey showed. But he did base his strategy a great deal on these results." The great majority of political scientists who have studied the relationship between presidential polling and public opinion concur. There is little evidence of pandering. Presidents, on the contrary, use polls to find the vocabulary that will resonate with the public. As analysts have noted, they engage in "crafted talk" that seeks to win the public over to the president's view, precisely what Woodrow Wilson would have hoped for. Presidents also use polling to find a way of speaking in public, which will demonstrate presidential awareness of and responsiveness to the public's preexisting concerns.

Political science has, in short, encouraged the activist presidency. That in turn has altered the relationship between the president and the vice president. Vice presidents have necessarily become more involved in governance. Because a vice president must instantly be as activist as his predecessor, should the president die in office, resign, or be removed by congressional impeachment and trial, the vice president must be as aware as possible of what the president knows and does not know. Vice presidents have, in fact, long met with the cabinet and since 1947 have been members of the National Security Council.

Presidents now also set the agenda of Congress, and they demand enactment of the "president's program." If the president leads by explaining himself regularly, and if a president is monitoring public opinion and also trying to get good advice on policy problems, then he is inevitably going to have a very full legislative agenda. This seems perfectly natural to us by now; however, that role cannot be found in the Constitution. In fact, article 2, section 3 reads only that "He shall from time to time give the Congress Information of the State of the Union and recommend to their consideration such Measures as he shall judge necessary and expedient."

Congressional government has become less central in American politics, as Wilson meant it to. But the presidency's evolution has helped to connect his use of the office to basic democratic standards: the rhetorical presidency enhances government by discussion, and presidential attention to public opinion enhances accountability. Presidential reliance on good policy advice means that executive decisions about "what to do" can be informed by expertise and competence.

These changes have nonetheless complicated the job of being the American president. Because they are constantly speaking to the people, presidents sometimes think that they can decisively shape public opinion—but the public has a mind of its own. Indeed, presidential monitoring of public opinion forces presidents and their advisers to acknowledge that firm public opinion on a wide range of issues already exists. The resort to expert advice on complex policy questions leads to yet another dilemma: the advice from specialists differs from how the public understands policy problems—and for presidents finessing that divergence can be challenging. The presidency's evolution has been good for American democracy, but its growth and change have resulted in an office that demands the utmost from its occupants.

Chapter 3
Congress and its bicameralism

The United States has one Congress, forged from two national legislatures—a 435-member House of Representatives and a 100-member Senate. First of all, article 1, section 7 of the Constitution requires them to work together to produce legislation. The Presentment Clause in article 1, section 7 reads, "Every Bill which shall have passed the House of Representatives and the Senate, shall, before it becomes a Law, be presented to the President of the United States." Second, binding these two legislatures into one Congress is the prohibition in article 1, section 5 on either chamber adjourning for longer than three days without the consent of the other chamber—and the ban in the adjournment clause on either chamber physically relocating itself. Third, the provisions (in article 1, sections 2 and 3) for House impeachment and Senate trial of a president, by majority and supermajority votes, further cement the two chambers. The Constitution gives the Congress a bicameral but interconnected design.

Both legislatures matter and are actually co-equal in part because the Founders designed them that way. Concerned that Congress might dominate the president and the Supreme Court, the

Founders opted for "different branches" with "different modes of election and different principles of action, as little connected with each other as the nature of their common functions and their common dependence on the society will admit." (The quotations come from the *Federalist*, an authoritative contemporary exposition of the Constitution written principally by James Madison and Alexander Hamilton with some assistance from John Jay.) This intention to strongly differentiate the two legislatures produced variants in size, terms of office, size of constituency, floor control, and constitutional responsibilities, such as advise-and-consent with respect to presidential treaty making and judicial appointment, in the Senate, and taxation in the House.

With every new biennial Congress, only a third of the Senate faces reelection for another six years. The entire House, in contrast, faces reelection for another two years. This arrangement was, at the Founding, meant to make the House sensitive to short-term shifts in constituent opinion and to give the Senate both a living memory and a long view of the national issues. The Senate could therefore play some part in foreign policy (through approval or rejection of treaties), in presidential staffing of the higher ranks of the executive branch, in the staffing of the federal judiciary, and in nominations by the president to fill Supreme Court vacancies. These tasks also explain why the Succession Act of 1792 made the Senate president pro tempore next in line to the presidency after the vice president for nearly a century—and today this officer can still become president if neither the vice president nor the Speaker of the House can serve.

As the United States became more democratic, the two legislatures acquired popular bases. A key institution that initially separated the Senate and the House was the indirect election of senators, via their state legislatures. But indirect election did not last very long. Although the Seventeenth Amendment (ratified in 1913) *formally* ended that "mode of election," indirect election effectively collapsed in many states well before the early twentieth century. The 1858 Illinois contest between Stephen Douglas and Abraham Lincoln for the Senate, which produced the great Lincoln-Douglas debates, was very much a popular canvas, for example. These rivals asked voters to vote for them via electing party slates in the Illinois legislature. The 1858 Illinois Senate contest thus mobilized the state's voters—an early example of de facto direct election.

Today one finds a mix of similarity and contrasts. Although both assemblies similarly represent American citizens according to where they reside, that is, in states, the two chambers have "different modes of election" in two senses. First, the members of the House come from districts with equal populations. This is why California, with the largest population in the country, has the largest state delegation in the House. In contrast, senators—but only two senators—represent the citizens of their entire state, regardless of the enormous inequalities in state populations. North Dakota has fewer people in it than a single House district in California, so it gets only one member in the House, but it also gets two senators. Several other states are in similar situations, such as Alaska, Montana, and South Dakota. The Senate is intentionally a very malapportioned legislature.

Nonetheless, because they are professional party politicians, senators and representatives behave quite similarly. They work equally hard at finding and talking with constituents, reaching out to business owners, chambers of commerce, Rotarians, newspaper editors, mayors, school boards, and not least the voters themselves at community centers, high schools, or even by giant conference calls. Senators are certainly as electorally vulnerable as their House colleagues. With the exception of small, sparsely populated states (the two Dakotas for example), senators represent jurisdictions with many more live or potentially salient issues to articulate, defend, or deflect than do representatives. There is more for electoral challengers to talk about in a statewide campaign—and more certainty that whatever they say will receive media coverage—for senators and senatorial campaigns attract much more media scrutiny than representatives and House elections do.

These two sets of professional politicians work within institutions of very different size: 100 members of the House versus 435 in the Senate (excluding special, nonvoting representatives from the District of Columbia, Puerto Rico, and the territories). That size difference coupled with roughly similar committees—the mini-legislatures that divide up the workload—generates a salient interchamber difference. Representatives are genuine policy specialists by virtue of relatively few assignments to relatively larger committees. They thereby acquire and supply real expertise to their House colleagues—about financial regulation, or defense procurement, or the implementation of environmental regulations. Senators, in contrast, have many more committee assignments, since 100 of them have to be shared among a committee system nearly as elaborate as that of the House. As a result they are more likely to be policy generalists with broad portfolios rather than specialists.

Leadership structures are a third dimension for comparison. The House has a constitutionally specified presiding officer—the Speaker—who is elected from the ranks of the House. She is able to control floor business and legislative scheduling through appointing loyal co-partisans to the Rules Committee, which defines the terms for a bill's floor consideration through detailed procedures laid out in "the rule" that must be voted and approved before a bill is considered.

In contrast, the Senate's constitutional presiding officer is not part of the body but is instead the vice president of the United States. Because the vice president has often belonged to the party that does *not* have a Senate majority in any given Congress, the Senate has resisted making the vice president a major part of the chamber's operation. In practice, the vice president usually presides only to break a tie vote. Also, there is nothing in the Senate equal to the Rules Committee of the House, that is, an issuer of procedural frameworks on which the chamber votes before considering legislative substance. Coordination of the Senate's business emerges instead from constant negotiations between the party leaders, the majority and minority leaders, positions that are not specified by the Constitution. Their coordinating roles first emerged late in the nineteenth century.

Today the two Senate party leaders resemble hostile twins bound together at the hip. They spend every legislative day negotiating accords on how to bypass the unwieldy written rules of the chamber: temporary interparty contracts that are known as "unanimous consent agreements." Both sides informally bargain with each other over how to proceed. In the House, in contrast, one side effectively tells the other side how it plans to proceed. It does this, for instance, when the majority-controlled Rules Committee reports the procedure that governs consideration of a bill to the floor—and the Speaker, the majority leader, and the majority whip then organize their side to approve the procedure (the rule) by majority vote.

The new filibuster

One institution that defines how the Senate's party leaders bargain with each other is the filibuster. The etymology of the word is a key to its political meaning and role within the Senate. Filibuster comes from the Spanish "filibustero," a word coined in the early nineteenth century to refer to roving soldiers of fortune. In the aftermath of the Spanish Empire's collapse, such would-be warlords, or "filibusteros," sailed from the United States, Europe, and Latin America with the aim of seizing land from weak governments in Mexico, the Caribbean, or Central America. They sought to create their own petty dictatorships. Somewhat similarly, a senator or a group of senators "filibuster" when they exploit the right that every senator has always had to be recognized for debate and to bring up any subject at all. In doing this, a filibustering senator or set of senators seize control of Senate business, greatly slowing the legislative process. A filibuster ends only when a supermajority of sixty senators vote to end it (which is known as "cloture").

This ancient set of privileges for an individual senator or a minority of the Senate interacts today with the ideological polarization of the American parties. The Senate has a left/right lineup, ranging from the most conservative senator to the most liberal, with many ideological gradations in between. The less ideologically extreme senators therefore become crucial to stopping filibusters. Those senators who can enable or block filibusters now influence the fate of legislation and presidential nominations to the federal judiciary, executive agencies, and independent regulatory commissions.

This does not mean, though, that these more moderate senators regularly act to end a filibuster after a long and dramatic debate by supplying the sixty votes needed for cloture. The filibuster instead refers today to a possibility, not an actual time-consuming event. The old-style filibuster made famous by Jimmy Stewart in the movie *Mr. Smith Goes to Washington*—holding the floor and talking nonstop in order to force the chamber to acquiesce in the policy demand of a passionate minority—disappeared some time ago.

The filibuster today is a *threat* by an individual or a minority of the chamber to slow the Senate down. The threat is real enough, but the majority only occasionally calls the bluff of those who threaten to produce what is now called a "live filibuster." Instead of forcing those who threaten to actually filibuster by talking on the floor, the majority simply holds a cloture vote: if it fails, it moves on.

For the most part individuals and the minority obstruct the majority routinely. In response the number of cloture votes has risen sharply. The Senate is operationally a supermajoritarian, sixty-forty legislature for all important matters that divide the parties. On matters that do not divide the parties the legislative process has instead slowed considerably and requires both successful cloture votes (that are often lopsided) and mutual toleration of the post-cloture debate period of thirty hours of debate.

Do the Senate and the legislative process have to work this way? Not at all. A partisan majority could, tomorrow, change the rules so that henceforth a simple party majority of as few as fifty-one could govern the Senate. But that would require a heroic struggle and leave very hard feelings. Moreover, every senator can imagine the political and electoral necessity, at some point in the future, of being among an influential minority of at least forty-one.

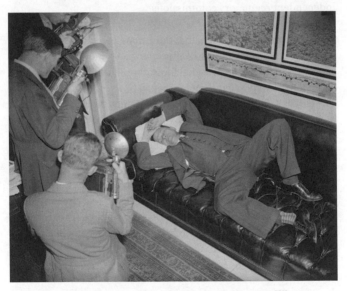

3. Senator Allen Ellender of Louisiana rests after a 1938 filibuster meant to weaken the law establishing the federal minimum wage. Filibusters no longer require physical stamina because the Senate is now too busy to wait them out; today senators make do with supermajority rule for major legislation.

Living with the filibuster-as-threat and the frequent cloture votes in the end is easier for all senators. As a legislature of one hundred they have figured out how to tolerate each other and their byzantine legislative practices. Also, in an era of intense electoral competition between the parties—and therefore heightened insecurity for all incumbents—every senator up for election at the next national election (about one-third of the chamber) has to get home for the long weekend to touch base with constituents. The others also need time to campaign and raise campaign funds.

All of this is rather new. Until quite recently the Senate was approximately as majoritarian as the House. The Senate simply had much fewer formal rules for implementing the principle of majority rule. Its small size facilitated a mix of informal procedural fluidity and de facto majority rule, which has often baffled and misled observers. In fact, the Senate did not even have a parliamentarian until 1937. But partisan majorities got their way most of the time, particularly if they were determined.

The majority governed the Senate and overcame the old-style "live" talkathon filibuster by holding its ground long enough until the minority conceded from fatigue. The majority shifted the time and energy to sustain a filibuster onto the minority. Gradually the minority, watching the majority (whatever its size) hold its ground day after day and sometimes for weeks, recognized that the majority was serious. So long as the majority pushed its preferred measures early in a congressional session and sustained its cohesion and patience in waiting out the minority, it could—and it did—run the Senate.

There are occasional echoes of this way of doing business. In late April 2010, Republicans threatened to filibuster the Dodd-Frank financial reform bill, so Democrats called their bluff. As cots were loudly set up outside the Senate's chamber, Republicans acquiesced and allowed the bill to move to the floor for debate.

In other words, the Senate has had *two* filibusters in its history. The old-style filibuster depended on sheer physical exertion and stamina, catnaps on cots in rooms off the floor, a desire to capture public attention as both sides on a contentious measure prepared to outlast each other, and grinding tests of a majority's determination to signal where *it* stood on a policy question. The new filibuster is different: it is an institutionalized assumption.

With the new filibuster there is essentially an informal agreement between the two parties. So long as the partisan minority numbers at least forty-one (which is most of the time), and so long as such a forty-one-member minority maintains its cohesion (meaning that the forty-first senator, whoever he or she is, does not defect), then that forty-one-member minority can—if it wants to— influence the majority on a wide range of legislative initiatives, on desired appointments to the federal judiciary, and on desired appointments to executive branch positions.

The working assumption of no defection for the forty-first (or for that matter the sixtieth) senator makes considerable sense, as well. Party loyalty is not guaranteed, to be sure. But the parties are polarized—and on many issues there simply is no ideological overlap. Of course, when the minority is larger than forty or forty-one, the minority's influence is all the greater.

Thus the new filibuster has transformed the Senate minority leader into a major political player in national American politics. In an important sense, the Senate minority leader and his colleagues normally exercise a kind of veto in the legislative process, in White House nominations to the federal judiciary, and in presidential appointments to federal agencies, including the Foreign Service.

This means that there is a new veto that cannot be found in the Constitution. The Constitution gives the president a *qualified* veto, one that can be overridden by a concurrent majority of two-thirds of the House and the Senate. It is the *only* veto in the Constitution. With it the president decisively shapes the legislative process, by signaling what he will accept or will not accept. From a formal-legal perspective, the extra-constitutional veto on legislation that is located now in the Senate is therefore located in the "wrong" branch and is the "wrong" kind. The Founders wanted only one veto, for the president, and they wanted a qualified veto, one that could be legislatively overridden through following a textually prescribed procedure. But in a Senate polarized from left to right, those who are willing to break filibuster threats have also become critical blockers and shapers of legislation and appointments within the separation of powers.

The new filibuster has another effect—on the size of a party's feasible policy agenda when it happens to control both chambers. When the same party holds a majority in both the House and the Senate, the Senate majority's policy agenda will be *smaller* than the House majority's policy agenda. This is because the Senate has a veto player that the House does not, and this can make members of the House majority rather angry. Congressman David Obey (D-Wisconsin), who served twenty-one consecutive terms, expressed deep irritation when he announced his plan to retire from the House at the end of the 111th Congress (2009–10): "I don't know what I will do next. All I do know is that there has to be more to life than explaining the ridiculous, accountability-destroying rules of the United States Senate to confused and angry and frustrated constituents." In other words, the House majority can enact what it prefers, so it can seem to do more than the Senate majority. But bicameralism means that the new limits on what the Senate majority can actually accomplish will *also* limit what their colleagues in the House can do when they are running the House—leaving them feeling very frustrated.

Chapter 4
The legislative-executive process

By design, the prospect of political stalemate is built into the American legislative-executive process. Presidents are elected on one calendar (no more than two terms of four years each); members of the House on another (every two years but without term limits); and senators on yet another (one-third up for reelection to a six-year term every two years, again without term limits). National officeholders represent and are accountable at various times to different constituencies.

The two political parties, Democrats and Republicans, can certainly overcome the possibility of deadlock if one of them controls the White House, the House, and the Senate at the same time. But rival ideologies—that is, competing, sometimes even opposite, ways of understanding such fundamental issues as taxing, spending, financial regulation, environmental policy—have reintroduced the tendency toward inaction that the Constitution facilitates. For example, there might be a Republican in the White House and Democrats running the Senate and the House, and *that* can lead to policy gridlock.

A Congress controlled by one party cannot easily make a president from the rival party accept policy that the president dislikes. Since

1789, thirty-six of forty-three presidents have exercised their veto authority more than 2,500 times. Congress's rate of override has been a little more than 4 percent—largely due to the two-thirds supermajorities in both houses required for override. By the same token and in contrast to chief executives in other countries, the president cannot dissolve Congress, nor can he propose budgets or legislation in a take-it-or-leave-it way.

Political scientists have long debated whether immobility is a glaring defect of the American legislative-executive process. In a now-classic finding first published in 1991 and updated in 2002, the political scientist David Mayhew showed that legislative productivity really does not depend on unified party control of the presidency and both houses of Congress. Mayhew devised an authoritative list of significant legislation for the House and the Senate since 1946 and identified many other forces besides unified control of national government that correlate with legislative productivity. He also mathematically tested whether unified party control by itself produced important laws at a higher rate. He weighed the presence of unified party control or divided government against such factors as change from the first half of a presidential term to the second half, presence or absence of a national "activist mood," of the kind that existed during the 1960s and 1970s when the idea of solving national problems was very much in the air, and variations in the budgetary situation (defined as surplus or deficit as a percentage of governmental outlays). Mayhew concluded that the presence of unified party control seems statistically unimportant. It does not "cause" higher legislative productivity.

An obvious possibility is that national government could be doing *more* without ideological polarization between Democrats and Republicans. Polarization can be measured, and it has varied and increased over the time period investigated by Mayhew, which runs from 1946 up to the 110th Congress, 2007–8 (Mayhew has since posted further updates on his website at Yale University, or http://pantheon.yale.edu/~dmayhew/data3.html). Thus one can simulate legislative productivity when polarization is lower than it currently is—precisely what another political scientist, Nolan McCarty, has done. His counterfactual simulation shows a growing gap after the mid-1970s, increasing from about one or two significant statutes per year to about fourteen or fifteen per year that the federal government might *otherwise* be producing.

The debate about gridlock will preoccupy American political scientists for some time. The risk of policy standoffs now hover constantly over American national politics. Partial governmental shutdowns, the threat of default on the national debt, and the threat of economically hazardous automatic tax increases and cuts in spending have all arrived like storms over Washington. The two parties now disagree fundamentally on taxing and spending measures.

Still, the parties have also invented new vehicles for making policy. One such device is the "omnibus" bill, a package containing an uncontroversial and desired core provision. Attached to the widely preferred "nucleus" of the bill are much more controversial positions, which would not survive on their own. The consensual core of the bill makes it easier to assemble floor majorities for the entire package.

Another innovation that also exploits the budget process in order to overcome the potential for policy deadlock is *budget reconciliation*. This is a once-technical device created in 1974 for closing a gap between annual budget targets, on the one hand, and the amounts appropriated for the thirteen basic appropriation categories of American national government on the other. It has metamorphosed since then into a powerful majoritarian tool, which has been used for difficult policy decisions nearly two dozen times. As a former parliamentarian of the Senate stated on national television in March 2010, "I would never use the term illegitimate when it comes to reconciliation. . . . It has been used for very large, major bills. It is a way of getting around the problem of the Senate filibuster."

4. Speaker of the House Nancy Pelosi (at podium), flanked by several powerful women committee chairs from the House of Representatives, appears at a press conference on the steps of the Capitol in June 2010 and calls on Senate Republicans to drop their obstruction of a Democratic jobs bill. Pelosi, a Democrat from California, served as Speaker from 2007 to 2010 and was the first woman to hold the office.

Written into the 1974 Budget and Impoundment Control Act, budget reconciliation was meant to tidy up the budget process as it came to an end every year. Any discrepancy between the aggregate result of the annual appropriations process and the budget target for that fiscal year could be achieved through tinkering with tax law. Social policy entitlements (Medicare, the mandated retirement health insurance system, for instance) could be paid for every year by fiddling with the entire set of budget numbers.

Any budget-reconciliation bill is "fast-tracked" through the Senate: it proceeds on a simple majority vote and under expedited debate. Any so-called "non-germane" amendment is forbidden. For instance, tacking on a new program to prevent child pornography—something that would otherwise easily win approval—is forbidden.

Democrats today seek to develop new social policy initiatives and find new sources of revenue. Republicans are deeply wedded to a program of tax cuts, the privatization of social policy, and reduction in government spending. This is the heart of the sharp interparty polarization that characterizes American national politics.

Under the circumstances, the "fast-track" features of budget reconciliation are a godsend to a majority in Congress. If one party controls both houses, it can come up with a huge new and procedurally protected bill, which reengineers tax and social policy even as it funds the government—and then it can dare the president in the opposite party to veto it. This is what Republicans tried to do in 1995 with President Bill Clinton when they passed an initial version of welfare reform that the President regarded as unhelpful for moving welfare recipients into the workforce. Or, if the same party controls both the White House and Capitol Hill, it does not need a clear supermajority in the Senate to do what it really prefers. This is how Republicans enacted tax cuts during the presidency of George W. Bush despite their manifest consequences for fiscal imbalance, or how the Democrats enacted the reform of health insurance that came to be known as "Obamacare."

Reconciliation bills are never simple 51 percent majority bills, and they often involve majorities close to or at the threshold for cloture in a filibuster, that is, sixty votes. The touch of supermajoritarianism in the use of the reconciliation procedure is due to a little-known check on openly partisan and policy uses of the budget reconciliation procedure—the "Byrd rule," after its author, the late Sen. Robert Byrd (D-West Virginia). Under the Byrd rule, which Congress adopted by statute in 1990, certain provisions in a budget reconciliation bill that are extraneous to the broad spirit of budget reconciliation as a *technical* device can be struck by a minority of forty-one—and the definition of "extraneous" in the statute is precise enough to give the Byrd rule teeth.

Nonetheless, determined partisan majorities have overcome the Byrd rule. The Senate parliamentarian usually defines the rule's application. The parliamentarian is, moreover, a career professional supported by a career staff. But the parliamentarian also serves at the pleasure of the Senate majority leader. Thus the majority sends representatives to the parliamentarian's office to discuss and negotiate any prospective ruling. These negotiations are colloquially called "Byrd baths." Essentially, the parliamentarian and the majority design a reconciliation bill so that it formally passes muster in the Senate.

Thus the Bush administration's tax cuts of 2001 and 2003, which, ironically, generated fiscal imbalance, were enacted via budget reconciliation. So was the "welfare reform" act of 1996. In addition to "Obamacare," several health care financing policies have been enacted via reconciliation: the Children's Health Insurance Program; access to a former employer's health insurance plan at higher individual premiums while a citizen changes jobs (the so-called COBRA benefit, after the Consolidated Omnibus Budget Reconciliation Act of 1986); and the federal requirement that all hospitals receiving Medicaid and Medicare financing must see *all* emergency room patients. Budget reconciliation means that not only the politics of taxing and spending but also the contentious area of health policy have come to partly resemble the other main policy area that is governed by "fast track" procedure, namely trade policy.

Nomination wars?

There are, however, areas of institutional interaction where one sees standoffs as often as getting things done. Party polarization and divided government can adversely affect presidential nominations and staffing of the executive branch and the federal judiciary. The exceptions are Supreme Court nominations and the military. Senators do not risk blocking a military appointment by the president—for example, a top commander for a U.S. military deployment. Court nominees never face filibusters once the Senate Judiciary Committee reports the nomination to the Senate floor. But a wide range of other presidential nominations are fair game.

There are about 1,230 top federal service appointments to be made by the president with the advice and consent of the Senate, including cabinet secretaries and such executives as the head of the Office of Legal Counsel in the Department of Justice. These top appointees lead a federal workforce of about 2.6 million.

The judiciary is also vulnerable. There are 677 district court judgeships in 94 federal judicial districts among the 50 states and the U.S. territories. In addition there are 179 courts of appeals judgeships. All are "article 3" judges—that is, they exercise the judicial power of the United States under article 3 of the Constitution, which creates the federal judiciary.

These two types of presidentially nominated officers differ. Bureaucrats and civil servants do not serve a life term as do most federal judges. On the contrary, a cabinet agency official will rarely serve a full presidential term. Nonetheless, both sets of officers get to their jobs through the Senate confirmation process.

The security clearance procedures (dating to the Eisenhower administration), the vetting, and the information-gathering parts of a nonjudicial nomination are already extremely onerous. The longer a nominee is forced by Senate delay to put his or her life on hold, after an arduous and intrusive clearance and vetting process, the more the prospect of serving one's country or one's president is likely to turn into an unnecessary headache. The nominee may decide to get rid of the headache by just giving up.

It has become steadily more difficult—though certainly not too difficult—for a president to assemble a government. Presidents have had to make creative use of the "recess appointment," getting an essential appointment in place when the Senate is not in session. During the 112th Congress (2011–13), Senate Republicans sought to prevent the Obama administration from making even recess appointments by holding the Senate continuously in session, as a pure formality, even though the Senate was not actually functioning. President Obama eventually decided to make the necessary appointments anyway, arguing that his constitutional responsibility to administer a government trumped such extreme Senate obstructionism.

As for nomination fights in judicial appointments, they too have become harder. They occur when the president must fill a judicial vacancy due almost always to retirement or death, though sometimes because of impeachment by the House and trial in the Senate. The average time normally required for confirmation of a judicial nominee has grown from about one month to six. Judicial appointments also become much slower during presidential election years as the president's opposition in the Senate runs out the clock in the hope that their party's nominee will have more appointments to fill.

Would the Founders be worried?

The Founding Fathers of 1787—Benjamin Franklin, Alexander Hamilton, James Madison, George Washington, and the other delegates to the Constitutional Convention in Philadelphia—did not anticipate the Senate's obstructionist institutions, such as the right to delay business by filibuster. The filibuster threat that hovers over all Senate business is today certainly constitutional—in the sense that the constant procedural delay is legitimate by virtue of its usage by both political parties.

The Constitution of 1787 now bears some resemblance, though, to the initial system of governance, the Articles of Confederation (1777). The Articles were widely considered a governmental failure because they did not address the evident need for effective national government. What the Founders put in place, they thought, was a workable institutional mix: enough checking and balancing to force national officeholders to start talking with each other in the language of public values and interests, even as they conduct much of their business according to majority rule. Today there is clearly less mutual deliberation than there used to be and more partisan appetite for making the other side look bad whenever possible.

The Founders might also wonder about the potential for abuse in congressional investigations. For example, the party control of Congress changed hands, from Republicans to Democrats, during the 110th Congress while a Republican, George W. Bush, was still president. The number of congressional investigations into executive branch operations during the first six months of the 110th Congress (2007–9) was more than 600. Earlier, though, Congress launched about 390 investigations during a comparable period, that is, the first six months of the previous, Republican-controlled Congress, the 109th (2005–7), For partisans, such as the new Speaker of the House, Nancy Pelosi (D-California) the point was to "drain the swamp" in a supposedly corrupt administration. Undoubtedly some of the stepped-up investigative effort was merited, but the cost to executive energy was considerable.

As democratic theorists in their own right, the Founders might today be a bit worried about the frictions in the legislative-executive process. Yet they would surely take comfort from the political scientist David Mayhew's 2011 finding that Congress generally responds to presidential leadership, particularly early in a presidency. In the post–World War II period, American presidents have gotten legislation that they strongly wanted about 61 percent of the time. Such an overall legislative success rate is quite close, it turns out, to how well chief executives in many different kinds of presidential democracies do with their legislative proposals.

Chapter 5
The Supreme Court

The chief justice and eight associate justices of the Supreme Court handle controversial social issues such as abortion, the decriminalization of gay sex, and the death penalty. They alter campaign finance law; they partly influence what presidents do in the area of the national security; they affect environmental policy; and they decide on national health insurance. In 2000 the Court settled a disputed presidential election. The Court is clearly a major player in national politics.

The Court plays this role by resolving real legal cases, with actual plaintiffs and defendants. As Justice Antonin Scalia remarked once during oral argument, "We are not a self-starting institution. We only disapprove of something when someone asks us to." The Court settles a case or controversy, between a plaintiff-appellant (*Brown*, to take a very famous plaintiff-appellant) and a defendant-appellee (*Board of Education of Topeka*). At least four justices (per the Court's "rule of four") must agree that the request for Court intervention, as framed, is worth considering. That agreement in turn is based on long-standing ideas shared among the justices about when the Court ought to respond, if at all, to a petition, and why. Only after they come to such an agreement does the Court authorize the parties to bring the case before the Court.

The Court often appears to function as America's last word on a subject: the Court decides at the end of a long legal sequence; it very often addresses fierce controversies; and its intervention into political disputes often seems very much like a constitutionally required *correction* of how other actors, earlier in the sequence, made their decisions.

As befits an institution that appears to be the nation's final word on weighty matters, the justices consciously strive to maintain the Court's dignity and internal collegiality. Since the tenure of Chief Justice Melville Fuller (1888–1910), the justices all shake hands with each other when they meet in their private deliberations— known as the "conference handshake."

Access to the Court is strictly regulated. Petitions and briefs are filed according to procedures that cannot be varied, and those who argue before the Court must be members of the Supreme Court Bar. They are highly credentialed lawyers—and often they are also government lawyers, such as the Solicitor General, who argues for the United States in cases in which it has an interest. Cameras are not allowed into the Court during oral argument, nor have the justices shown any inclination to respond to the frequent proposals that the Court's proceedings be televised. Personally lobbying a justice or one of the recent law school graduates who clerk for the justices simply never happens because it would be met with hostility.

Justices of the Supreme Court are themselves intensely aware of this rather thick institutional and professional boundary between the Court and the rest of the political system. They regard joining the Court as a stringent test of their skills and intelligence. One former associate justice has likened it to "walking through a tidal wave." Another associate justice has confessed to being "frightened to death for the first three years." Such anxious reactions are consistent with the idea that the Court has solemn and vitally important responsibilities to the nation as a whole.

5. Supreme Court associate justice Elena Kagan takes the oath of office in 2010, administered by Chief Justice John G. Roberts Jr. (right) on a Bible held by counselor to the chief justice Jeffrey P. Minear. Kagan was nominated by President Barack Obama and confirmed by a Senate margin of 63–37.

A typical scenario that leads the Court to hand down an opinion begins with a case or controversy coming into the federal judicial system. Article 3, section 2 of the Constitution states, "The judicial Power shall extend to all Cases" and "to Controversies" arising under the Constitution and the laws of the United States. The Court considers an appellant's petition, filed at the office of the Court's clerk, asking that the Court order a lower court to have the materials of the case brought before the Court. If the Court accepts the petition and issues its order to the court below (known as a *writ of certiorari*), it schedules briefing and oral argument, and it also accepts "friend of the Court" briefs, typically from a wide range of interest groups. These briefs alert the justices that the Court's agreement to hear a case or controversy, and its decisions, are being closely monitored.

The Court bides its time, however, in addressing controversial issues. It can do this because the Court controls its own docket.

The Judiciary Act of 1925 abolished automatic appeals to the Court for the vast majority of cases—and it was in the Act's wake that the informal "rule of four" emerged within the Court. One happy result is that the Court is not overwhelmed by the literally thousands of petitions that arrive at the office of its clerk every year. Instead, the Court can choose whether and how best to address legal questions that also will influence public policy.

This process has come to be known as *judicial review* (to use a term that came into use around 1900). Judicial review is consideration by the entire Court of practices, actions, or decisions taken by the federal government or state and local governments, or by private actors with a duty to obey a federal statute that they resist as flawed. Judicial review means that someone—a person or a branch of American government who (or which) has standing to object to a decision, action, or behavior—has found a successful judicial "frame." That is, the objectionable governmental or private action has been posed, compellingly, as a matter of constitutionally improper action. Or it has been posed to the Court as an incorrect and jurisprudentially significant misapplication of a statute or legal rule.

Then, a majority of the Court (and about a third of the time the entire Court) will come down on one side or another of the controversy. In doing so the majority or the Court partly accepts how one of the parties to the dispute framed the issues while also partly reframing the issues from the Court majority's perspective.

Very rarely is *all* of what is at stake decided. Cases or controversies before the Court involve legislation or ordinances that have many parts, or complex patterns of compliance or noncompliance with laws. Almost always the objection that the Court has decided to entertain and decide is a *partial* objection. The decision for the Court gives the reasons for the decision by majority or unanimous vote. There are also written disagreements with the decision, known as *dissents*, and there may be partial or full *concurrences* with either the Court's decision or with one of the dissents, but on separate grounds.

The decisions and opinions build on previous decisions. The decisions partly rest on citations and summaries of other Supreme Court and federal court decisions. But their authors ground them not only in a reading of what their predecessors have done in similar or related cases but also in principles of statutory or constitutional interpretation. They are embedded within a coherent legal framework that their authors use to guide the reasoning in their decisions.

None of this is divorced from the justices' underlying political values, to be sure. The justices are in fact predictably "conservative" or "liberal," and they understand that they are making public policy in a "conservative" or "liberal" way. They may pick and choose, too, among the facts and arguments offered to the Court by those who have submitted "friend of the Court" briefs on either side of a case. The difference between what the justices do and what members of Congress do is that the justices must openly and carefully connect what they write to legal and constitutional traditions. They must also clearly address the claims and arguments of the parties before the Court. Indeed, the justices believe that they are often required to make decisions that they personally would not agree with.

Members of Congress, in contrast, while they certainly take constitutional and legal traditions into account, also weigh public opinion, the arguments that they have heard from constituents, lobbyists, and executive branch officials, the information that they have gathered through committee hearings and staff research, their deliberations with their colleagues, and their own partisan perceptions of the issues and of current events. Members of Congress thus bring a fairly broad mix of considerations into lawmaking. Judging, in contrast, is deeply and consciously shaped by the existing law.

The educative rationale

In a way the Court's role is quite puzzling. Why in a democracy do nine unelected men and women, serving for life on a high court, seem to function as a nation's final say? One leading and widely accepted answer is that judicial review is broadly educative. Having a fundamental charter such as the Constitution means that some set of actors must announce what that charter and associated texts (statutes and previous Court decisions) mean—and that institution is the Supreme Court. No other officials in Washington, D.C., constantly think about the Constitution and the vast body of judicial, presidential, and congressional commentary on its meaning.

Elected politicians certainly recognize this. Contrary to conventional wisdom, Senate confirmation hearings for nominees to the Court are *not*—taken as a whole—what Justice Elena Kagan once colorfully labeled a "vapid and hollow charade." A twentieth-century innovation that has paralleled the increased policy-making salience of the Court, confirmation hearings are actually marked by rather candid, wide-ranging discussions back and forth, between senators and nominees, over such matters as judicial philosophies, the merits of famous decisions, and how the nominees think about the role of a Supreme Court justice. They are not perfect discussions, and there are indeed evasive answers. But confirmation hearings arouse broad public discussion for weeks.

The Court's justices, through their lengthy and closely reasoned decisions, renew and update national support for, among other institutions and practices, free speech, separation of church and state—and, more generally, the separation-of-powers structure between the federal, state, and local governments. Their decisions rightly attract public attention. When they gain notice many citizens will be forced to think about what the Constitution and judicial review actually mean. Surveys show that citizens pay considerable attention to the Court and assess whether its decisions are, as the citizens see them, liberal or conservative.

As Eugene Rostow, a Yale University law professor, once wrote, "The Supreme Court is, among other things, an educational body, and the Justices are inevitably teachers in a vital national seminar." The Court's insulation from electoral politics, the recruitment of men and women with distinguished careers as government lawyers, in public interest litigation, or as judges, and the life tenure of appointments to the Court are especially relevant features of the Court as an institution. They free the Court's members to engage in good-faith jurisprudence without fear of retribution for making decisions that might displease the president, members of Congress, or angry citizens.

Admirers of the Court's educative role will note how irritating Supreme Court justices can be to the presidents who nominated them. Dwight D. Eisenhower was famously appalled by Earl Warren's evolution into a rights-oriented liberal after he was appointed chief justice. He had been the law-and-order governor of California and an avid advocate of President Franklin D. Roosevelt's internment of Japanese Americans during World War II. David Souter—another appointee who turned out to be quite liberal—must have left President George H. W. Bush shaking his head.

Indeed, the Court has acted when politicians seem stuck or afraid to act. The classic example is *Brown v. Board* (shorthand for two related decisions in 1954 and 1955), ordering the desegregation of the nation's public schools with "all deliberate speed." Members of the Court try to develop public support for their role—and they act accordingly. They know that they are potentially "countermajoritarian" when they see an issue differently than a majority or an impassioned minority of the public. They anticipate reactions from parts of the public or from the president or Congress in especially controversial areas.

The policy-making court

Many political scientists, however, dissent from the educative rationale for the Supreme Court. They instead consider judicial review a form of national policy making. Many different kinds of unelected, appointed officials—for instance, the chairman of the Federal Reserve (the central bank of the United States) or the Securities and Exchange Commission—make policy. In this analysis, the Supreme Court is just one among several insulated policy-making bodies.

If there is policy making, then there is conflict. Different members of the Court regularly see varying implications in the language of the Constitution, of previous Court decisions, and of federal statutes. There are often narrow liberal or conservative majorities, and justices on the losing end of a decision for the Court will issue bitter, denunciatory dissenting opinions. Not always content with written dissent, they sometimes also offer oral dissent, reading portions of their opinion out loud from the bench on the day that the decision for the Court is announced, thus (as one newspaper story had it) "supplementing the dry reason on the page with vivid tones of sarcasm, regret, anger, and disdain."

The Court's associate justices and its chief justice are rarely unanimous in deciding high-profile cases. A particularly clear case of political division on the Court is *Bush v. Gore* (2000). The Court's five conservative justices essentially stacked future appointments to the Court, one scholar of the Court has suggested, by throwing their authority behind the conservative presidential candidate, George W. Bush, and assuring his assumption of the presidency. Based on the kind of nominations President Bush would make, the conservative majority assured the dominance of the Court by conservative judges.

Conflict is indeed constant on the Court, and it exists because those who appoint justices to the Court—the president, with the consent of a majority of the Senate—settle on nominees affiliated with one political party or the other. Beyond the Court, in the White House and in the Senate, which confirms White House nominations to the Court, there are strong and distinct partisan preferences over what kinds of justices to recruit to the Court. The nomination and appointment processes are therefore sometimes harsh and polarized.

Moreover, resistance to Supreme Court decisions is actually pervasive in American politics. *Brown v. Board of Education* (1954) struck down state laws requiring racially segregated public schools. Yet the public schools of the United State are today de facto as racially segregated as they once were. In the years since the decision in the mid-1950s, millions of whites have simply abandoned public school systems, or they have moved to affluent, predominantly white school districts. Given the wealth gap between whites and blacks, and the subtle and not-so-subtle ways in which residential segregation is informally defended in much of the United States, there are not very many black students in affluent suburbs. In effect, and in reality, there has been more than half a century of white backlash against *Brown*.

Resistance to Court decisions means that judicial review in a particular policy area is sometimes a dance without an end. The obvious example is abortion. In *Roe v. Wade* (1973) a substantial majority of the nine-person Supreme Court held that women have the freedom and right to abort fetuses before the last trimester of pregnancy. Majorities on the Court have since gradually accepted efforts by state legislatures and the so-called pro-life members of Congress to regulate (and, some would say, to thereby restrict) the access of women to that right. These other actors have imposed counseling requirements and prevented federal funding of abortion; successive majorities of the Court have treated these changes as reasonable regulations that do not diminish the right. The Court as an institution has thus been interacting with state legislatures and Congress and jointly regulating a major policy domain for nearly forty years—and continually recasting the nature of the reproductive right that a majority announced in 1973.

The political uses of judicial review

Judicial review can also be very useful to those who are not on the Court. Politicians have very strong incentives, for some issues, to pass the buck to the Supreme Court and move controversies out of legislative-executive processes. Congress could, for instance, write a national law guaranteeing the right to abortion. If it did, though, most of the Congress would be retired at the next election, ending careers that members have carefully managed for a long time. No pro-choice member of Congress will say on the record that electoral insecurity prevents Congress from writing a national abortion rights statute. But this is why pro-choice members have done little to directly reinforce the abortion right since *Roe*.

The decision in *Bush v. Gore* (2000)—in which a majority of the Court awarded the presidency, in effect, to George W. Bush— would be inconceivable if politicians did not prefer judicial adjudication. Rather than allow resolution of the electoral crisis to occur in Congress, as contemplated by the 1887 Electoral Count Act, both the Gore camp and the Bush camp agreed to resolve their dispute within the framework of national judicial review of Florida's electoral count. Judicial review often results from major players in the political system *preferring* judicial resolution to some alternative process.

The preference for judicial review will vary for different groups and political parties. Some people like it some of the time—and they loudly sing its praises. Those who dislike what the Court is doing at any particular time will try to change its docket or to constantly test the strength of the Court's support for a divisive precedent (as with the long line of cases after *Roe v. Wade* that are meant to test the Court's support for it). Members of Congress will introduce bills to "curb" the Court by changing its jurisdiction, a tactic allowed by the Constitution. Sometimes presidents or presidential candidates will forcefully criticize the Court for its rulings.

Nonetheless, the Court can issue divisive rulings because there is a coalition *off* the Court—comprising politicians, organized groups, and citizen activists—that will strongly support what the Court's majority does. The Court can function as the last word because it has allies who *want* it to have the last word. The Court's opponents are forced to wait until they can get a chance, through retirement from the Court, to influence the composition of the Court.

Thus the Court is a participant in ideological and partisan disputes. Almost everyone in American politics wants the weight of judicial opinion on its side at some time or another. The Court is allowed and sometimes explicitly invited to play a central role because it is politically useful to different people at different times.

In the end the best way to resolve these contrasting views of the Supreme Court—educative versus political—is to frame the Supreme Court's role as a hybrid of politics and law. The Court's role reflects the larger dualism of American politics: it is indeed a key element in the meshing of constitutional and extra-constitutional processes. The Court's quasi-political role constantly introduces constitutional thinking and a constitutional voice into American politics. If the Court were *not* quasi-political, if it lacked allies and partnerships with other branches and with players in the party system, then it could hardly play an educative role over time. No one would be listening to it. Those who are not on the Court want to listen to it, and they want to hear what it has to say—even if they disagree—precisely because it is a major player in policy making and politics.

Chapter 6
Bureaucracy

The American public generally dislikes bureaucracy—largely because many citizens believe that government wastes taxpayer money. Somewhat paradoxically, Americans also take the competence of government agencies for granted. One symbol of such capability—paper currency—is in every wallet or purse. Its printing, orderly circulation, and physical use depend on the expertise of employees in the Department of the Treasury and the Federal Reserve System. Also, there are more than 700,000 domestic commercial passenger flights each month, courtesy of the Federal Aviation Administration's orderly flight environment for air travel. And when Americans swallow prescription drugs for anxiety, depression, cholesterol control, or hypertension, their confidence in their relative safety and efficacy can be traced to the Food and Drug Administration (FDA) of the Department of Health and Human Services.

National bureaucracies have been essential for American commerce: the Census Bureau's data troves aid commercial marketing; the Defense Advance Research Projects Agency did the pioneering work that led to the Internet; the Department of Agriculture, through its extension service, steadily improved agricultural productivity over the twentieth century.

6. Lucy Alexander, a home economics specialist and food tester at the Department of Agriculture, ca. 1930. The Department of Agriculture published bulletins by Alexander on proper food preparation as part of its mission to promote nutrition and healthy diets—an example of how government agencies consciously cultivate public support.

The democratic requirement that public debate and discussion be meaningful depends on bureaucratic efficacy; otherwise debates about the direction of government would be inconsequential. When presidential candidates promise voters that they will fix the economy, they and their audiences assume that new governmental action might indeed affect macroeconomic performance in desired ways. Although some schools of economics vigorously (and quite cleverly) dispute the premise, other studies show that these are not hollow promises. Government economists working at the Federal Reserve, the Council of Economic Advisors, the National Economic Council, the Office of Management and Budget, and the Congressional Budget Office produce competent forecasts and reasonably good models, and they work with solid statistics. These strengths inform governmental steering of the economy.

Some bureaucracies do terrifyingly difficult things—such as prevent the accidental launch of American nuclear weapons, or prevent "meltdown" at nuclear reactors. Privatization and "marketization" could never completely handle such tasks.

Despite suspicions concerning governmental waste, Americans in fact hold discerning views of agency performance. About 80 percent of Americans think that the U.S. military is doing an excellent or good job, and about 70 percent take the same view of the Postal Service. About 57 percent say the same about National Aeronautics and Space Administration (NASA) and the Federal Bureau of Investigation (FBI), and 62 percent like the performance of the Centers for Disease Control. In contrast, the Food and Drug Administration (of the Department of Health and Human Services), the Department of Homeland Security, and the Veterans Administration all get ratings in the low 40s. These data suggest a public thinking about governmental competence, an awareness that coexists with its simultaneous diffuse discontent about wasteful expenditure.

The efficiency of delegation

In tacitly partnering with bureaucracies, even as they complain about the partnership, politicians and citizens implicitly rely on an efficiency in the economist's sense: *the efficiency of delegation*. That efficiency is ubiquitous. Unless they ardently believe in alternative medicine, most people delegate their medical care to their doctors. Unless they strongly prefer home schooling, people delegate the education of their children to trained teachers. Such delegation frees up time to do other things with one's skills and energies.

Similarly, the delegation of complex and important tasks to specialized, energetic bureaucracies expand what politicians can try to do and what citizens can expect from politicians. Delegation to people with expertise expands politicians' tools for controlling or influencing the processes that citizens want them to direct, regulate, somehow make a dent in, or stop altogether, such increasing rates of inflation and unemployment, widespread narcotics abuse, or water pollution.

The president and Congress have regularly created new bureaucracies to respond to a new collective commitment or to address a new risk or problem. The Department of Justice was established in 1870 in part to allow forceful federal implementation of civil and voting rights for African Americans in the wake of emancipation and the ratification of the Civil War and Reconstruction Amendments to the Constitution. Just a few months after the first Earth Day demonstration by some 20 million citizens, President Nixon issued an executive order that created the Environmental Protection Agency, building it out of several existing agencies. After 9/11, Congress and President Bush assembled the Department of Homeland Security out of several dozen existing bureaucracies.

Government agencies make mistakes, though, and sometimes experience spectacular failures; for example spaceship missions blowing up on launch or not preventing 9/11 or Pearl Harbor. Macroeconomic management, which can draw on good data and a well-developed social science, can also be quite risky. The Federal Reserve's top decision-makers misunderstood the onset of the Great Depression and made it much worse by tightening the money supply, which precipitated a collapse of the banking system by the time Franklin D. Roosevelt was inaugurated. The belief within the Fed that the housing bubble in the first decade of the twenty-first century would be self-correcting, and the inconsistent handling by the Treasury and the Fed of the financial crisis of 2008, helped put the American economy into a free fall and brought the country startlingly close to a second Great Depression.

Sometimes politicians push bureaucracies to cut corners and take risks. For example, the former Minerals Management Service (MMS) of the Department of the Interior is charged with the supervision of offshore drilling. A defective regulatory process led to the 2010 Gulf of Mexico oil spill. But the MMS had been required to issue permits in thirty days, and Congress supplied it with just sixty inspectors for four thousand offshore rigs. More broadly, there was citizen demand for cheap oil and bipartisan consensus on testing the limits of drilling technology. When these elements met a company known for cutting corners, British Petroleum, even when it drilled so-called wildcat wells—wells drilled in conditions never previously tested—the stage was set for a disaster and its ensuing drama of finger-pointing, blame assessment, and investigative journalism.

Thus recrimination and scandal regularly disturb the partnership between citizens and politicians on the one hand and bureaucracies on the other. Politicians, presidents in particular, may find themselves holding their breath and wondering if their approval ratings or careers are at stake in bureaucratic performance. Yet this sort of suspense is built into the partnership. The men and women in government agencies cannot banish risks or perfectly optimize their many and conflicting mandates; they only cope with them.

The federal government must and does partner with "contractors and grantees" who (in the words of a public administration scholar) "provide talent it cannot recruit, specialized services it cannot produce, competition it cannot generate among its own organizations, and equipment that it cannot and should not build itself." But that differs from giving up on the basic efficiency of delegation: it is simply another kind of delegation.

In addition to expanding what politicians can reasonably promise or publicly debate, and what citizens can expect from government, the partnership with bureaucracy (and bureaucratically supervised contractors) has another vital consequence. Having competent bureaucracy strengthens the Constitution. Bureaucracy helps to establish the dualism that defines American politics—the meshing of constitutional and extra-constitutional institutions and processes.

The president of the United States simply could not exercise the office if he had to personally superintend the Joint Chiefs of Staff every day. Members of Congress could hardly do anything else if they personally managed the implementation of, say, anti-narcotics statutes, or personally handled Social Security payments to the elderly. Indeed, the officials described in articles 1 and 2 of the Constitution—the president, senators, and representatives— could not *be* who they are today without the delegation efficiency of bureaucracies.

Bureaucracies must be given clear instructions according to American constitutional law. They cannot wholly supplant the basic executive and legislative functions described in those constitutional articles. But within the rather loose boundaries of the so-called non-delegation doctrine, the delegation efficiency of bureaucracies facilitate a vital partnership. They link modern government and the constitutionalism that was first devised in the eighteenth century.

Political footballs

Yet the fundamental harmony of constitutional modernization and public administration also encompasses constant political conflict with and within bureaucracies. This is particularly true with agencies that are regulatory. Regulation systematically influences the behavior of firms and citizens. The idea is thereby to achieve certain valuable public goals—acceptable levels of air or water pollution, for example, or safe workplaces. Thus agencies will issue rules. Some administrative actions may be unreasonable; they will and should invite oversight and discussion.

There is, of course, a fine line between worthwhile and ill-considered pressures from the White House and Congress. The White House, Congress, the courts, citizens, special interest groups, and the media all debate where that line is. As a consequence, government agencies in the United States continually respond to many competing players in bureaucratic politics.

The National Labor Relations Board (NLRB) is one agency where interference happens regularly. If a Democratic president appoints a new member of the NLRB, he typically wants that appointee to decide the scores of appeals from the NLRB's administrative courts in ways that strengthen the National Labor Relations Act's protections for collective bargaining and against unfair labor practices by employers (such as firing employees for trying to organize a union). Democrats and organized labor want a pro-labor NLRB. But a Republican president, in contrast, may want an appointee to be less pro-labor. A Republican president and organized business will want the NLRB to see the law of collective bargaining from the perspective of management and business owners.

Yet the president, his party, and the allies of that party hardly decide the matter entirely. If the Senate strongly disagrees with the president, then a substitute NLRB nomination may be necessary. The nomination success of the president's preferred candidate will depend critically on whether his own party controls the Senate and by what majority.

Another football that is often in play is the Environmental Protection Agency (EPA). During the administration of President George W. Bush, the EPA refused to accept regulatory responsibility for climate change. It did not have to. Republicans enjoyed control of Congress for most of the Bush presidency. Eventually a number of states, supported by environmental groups, sued the EPA for failing to enforce the 1970 and 1990 Clean Air

Acts by directly regulating carbon emissions. By statute, Congress provides for judicial review of agency decisions in most policy areas—which makes the appeals courts and the Supreme Court yet another set of principals. After losing at the federal circuit level, the states then petitioned the Supreme Court for review. In *Massachusetts v. Environmental Protection Agency* (2007) the Supreme Court narrowly held, 5–4, that the EPA was required to regulate greenhouse gases. But, taking seriously the idea that the executive branch is the president's business and no one else's, the EPA and the Bush administration simply ignored the ruling. Here they had a crucial 1984 Supreme Court ruling on their side: *Chevron U.S.A., Inc. v. National Resources Defense Council, Inc.,* which held that agency decisions should be accorded considerable deference (a rule subsequently dubbed "*Chevron* deference").

When the Obama administration came into office, the EPA issued new rules to comply with the Supreme Court decision. Republican senators who agreed earlier with the idea of "*Chevron* deference" now saw matters at the EPA in a different light. Sen. Lisa Murkowski (R-Alaska) persuaded the Senate majority leader to permit a vote on a resolution of disapproval under the little-used Congressional Review Act of 1996. As she put it, "The Clean Air Act was written by Congress to regulate criteria pollutants, not greenhouse gases, and its implementation remains subject to oversight and guidance from elected representatives. We should continue our work to pass meaningful energy and climate legislation, but in the meantime, we cannot turn a blind eye to the EPA's efforts to impose back-door climate regulations with no input from Congress." In the end, the vote failed. But the vote was clearly a shot across the bow of the EPA.

Strategies of control

The administrative state has been around long enough for the main players, namely Congress, presidents, political parties, and interest groups, to have developed strategies for pressuring bureaucracies. Many agencies have advisory commissions—there are about a thousand such commissions in all—that promote direct discussion at public hearings between constituencies of an agency and their senior officials. Moreover, the Administrative Procedure Act of 1946 requires agencies to give plain notice of what they plan to do and to formally solicit comments from interested parties. Between the advisory commissions and the Administrative Procedure Act, a supply of precise information about agency behavior is guaranteed. Interest groups affected by what agencies do will alert congressional allies, demanding, for instance, a congressional oversight hearing or asking members of Congress to send letters of concern to agency officials. For these reasons some scholars argue for a "congressional dominance" view of the administrative state, by which they mean that Congress effectively monitors what bureaucracies are doing by triggering a constant and large volume of reporting about their work to Congress and the public.

Presidents, on the other hand, also have strategies. The president has hundreds of important policy-making nominations with which to assert control over federal agencies. Presidents have also pushed for executive branch reorganizations. Increasingly, they issue "signing statements" when they sign legislation, thereby announcing that they may modify congressional controls. They appoint "czars" in the White House whose jobs are to peer inside agencies under the president's authority and figure out how to use them or get around them. For several decades presidents have centralized "regulatory review" inside the White House, requiring that agencies must report to the president about what they intend to do and why. The clearinghouse for this information is the White House Office of Information and Regulatory Affairs. Presidents and their czars can also assign officials loyal to the White House to agencies that they want to monitor closely.

Bureaucrats themselves struggle to escape such controls, or at least to manage them in ways that allow them considerable discretion.

As one congressional staffer told a political scientist, "One of the ironies of Washington is that you get agencies who believe that Congress has, or should have, no role in what they're doing." Bureaucratic leaders present at the creation and early years of an agency are often particularly talented at gaining autonomy. They may be able to create a sense of mission, an organizational culture, and a string of accomplishments that effectively ward off would-be overseers. One notable case was the FBI during the tenure of its longtime director J. Edgar Hoover.

Bureaucratic autonomy is conditional, however. The Federal Reserve, for example, was abruptly subjected to direct control by President Franklin D. Roosevelt in the wake of its policy mistakes from 1929 to1933, during the presidency of Herbert Hoover. It took decades for Fed bureaucrats to regain autonomy for America's central bank. At the zenith of this effort, during the chairmanship of Alan Greenspan, the men and women of the Federal Reserve system were treated as wizards by members of Congress. Then suddenly, in 2009 and 2010, in the wake of the housing bubble's collapse and the Fed's rescue of irresponsible financial institutions, the 111th Congress vigorously sought new ways to scrutinize the Fed's decisions, and the central bank mounted a public relations campaign to advertise that it was in fact transparent and accountable.

The development of bureaucratic government has given rise to new forms of interbranch, partisan, and group struggle carried out on the terrain of government agencies. The efficiency of delegating complex tasks to experts will expand the degree to which presidents and members of Congress can function as executives and representatives. But those actors therefore have strong incentives to monitor bureaucracies or to welcome monitoring by groups, courts, and the media—and also to directly control and sometimes micromanage bureaucracies.

Chapter 7
Public opinion and its influence

Most Americans struggle to grasp public affairs and politics. At least 60 percent of the public has consistently told the American National Election Studies (conducted at the University of Michigan) that it agrees with the statement, "Sometimes politics and government seem so complicated that a person like me can't really understand what's going on." Busy with work, child-rearing, and managing their households, Americans have little spare time or energy for following what government and politicians do. There are exceptions, especially those who are passionately concerned about global warming or Social Security or any other burning issue. The term for them is "issue publics." But most people are, quite understandably, politically inattentive most of the time.

Political scientists thus worry and argue about citizen rationality and competence. When academic survey researchers first peered closely at the American voter in the late 1940s and the 1950s, they came away astounded by how little ordinary people seemed to know about politics. Nothing in the intervening years has changed that finding. Recently political scientists have also become interested in how certain thinking patterns will affect how citizens assess their policy choices. One such pattern is so-called loss aversion, that is, having an irrationally hard time trading something already in one's possession for something of equal value. This is one reason why the privatization of Social Security is very difficult for a politician to push with any success, as President Bush tried to do after his reelection in 2004.

There is also concern about the well-informed and highly educated citizen with a strong partisan leaning. Because that person is very well educated, he or she knows clearly what is at stake in minimizing (or embracing) established facts about which there is political contention—whether there were weapons of mass destruction in Iraq after all (there were none), or whether human activity is significantly altering the world's climate (it is). The person's educational attainment provides the cognitive skills for "rationalizing." Partisanship tells him or her what side of the issue to grasp, and that person's cognitive skills can find ways to downplay public discussion of disagreeable facts.

So how can—how *do*—men and women who do not pay much attention to politics (and even when they do pay attention fall prey to such cognitive biases as loss aversion and rationalization)—influence government? How can they control those who represent them in (and who govern them from) physically or psychologically distant marble palaces of legislation, justice, or administration? A rather surprising channel for popular control is media dissemination of the findings of scientific opinion surveys.

Survey techniques come from statistical and mathematical advances dating to the late nineteenth and early twentieth centuries in England, Norway, and Poland. These subsequently diffused to American academia, particularly at Iowa State University and the University of Chicago, where they were married to a strong interest in discovering attitudes—an interest that found its way into the U.S. Department of Agriculture during the New Deal, where top bureaucrats wanted to know what farmers thought about New Deal farm programs. The academic and governmental strands were fused to techniques of rapid in-person interviewing and data collection about consumer tastes pioneered by marketing researchers on Madison Avenue, such as George Gallup. During World War II the National Opinion Research Center set up shop at the University of Chicago. Columbia University in Manhattan (located not far from Madison Avenue) also became a center for field research into the attitudes and levels of information that drove voter choice. The federal government, through the National Science Foundation, laid further foundations for the development of modern academic survey research at the University of Michigan, which has been home to the American National Election Studies since the 1950s.

As survey research spread into newspapers, major broadcast networks, and political campaigns, more technical improvements occurred. The professional community for the assessment of strengths, weaknesses, and ethics in polling also became highly developed. At one time that community was simply the journal *Public Opinion Quarterly*, established in 1935, but it now comprises regular conferences, professional associations, and blogs that publicize bad polling.

The rise of the survey has recast democratic accountability. Millions of citizens do not have to do anything in order for a highly stylized version of what they might think about policy questions to be heard at the top. Tiny fractions of compatriots, gathered in representative samples, speak for the public as they respond to surveys. The print, broadcast, and digital media subsequently publicize "what the American public thinks" to politicians, officials, commentators, and advocacy groups.

These samples of about eight hundred to two thousand individuals are broadly (though never fully) representative. Each respondent in the sample is drawn from a population in which everyone has a fairly equal chance of being contacted and interviewed. There are limits to this sampling: most Americans have a landline, cell phone, or smart-phone, but some sub-populations do not. High-speed Internet access is expensive for a household. Thus Internet surveys have to be weighted by complex algorithms in order to mimic the randomization factor in telephone surveys. But to a considerable degree survey samples are social and political mirrors.

Those who write survey questions or create Internet survey widgets design them so that analysts can get interpretable responses from the surveys that can be widely circulated and accepted as free from bias. The questions used in the good surveys—and there are now a few dozen—are subject to rigorous professional review for neutrality and efficacy. Questions about public policy, assessments of public officials, and the direction of the country are asked the same way year after year. As a result, opinion change or continuity over time can be observed, and the causes of shifts in responses can be analyzed and debated.

Government agencies, newspapers, and broadcast media networks, universities, foundations, and privately owned research firms all field such surveys. Most people never take part in them, but new slivers of the citizenry constantly participate. Two scholars who assembled a database of policy preference surveys from 1935 to 1990 found more than ten thousand policy preference questions. Of these, 1,128 had been asked in identical form over those decades.

Only a very small percentage of citizens know any specific survey results, but politicians pay close attention to the news about polls. They and their staffs read print media, download surveys from websites, subscribe to specialized reporting services (Capitol Hill and state and local governments support a large number of periodicals about the people and issues in them), and they have several televisions operating at all times in their offices during the day.

Media reports on the results of opinion surveys about public figures and policy issues generate an environment of popular signals, signals about the job the president is doing, trust in government, health care reform, American military interventions, and other issues. That environment operates between elections and in addition to the messages conveyed to officeholders by lobbyists or through individual citizens' irate, alarmed phone calls to a senator's office on Capitol Hill or letters to the president.

There is no requirement that politicians respond to these signals, even if they (or, in the fine phrase of one opinion scholar, the messages from "numbered voices") are clear and unmistakable. Yet the signaling environment of constant polling creates, for people in public office, several choices where once there were none. Politicians can choose to ignore the opinion evidence, or they can take the opinion evidence partly into account, or they can try carefully to think through what the evidence means and act accordingly. Finally, they can try to persuade citizens to think differently about policy and politics.

Therein lies the innovation in popular control brought about by scientific surveys. Political representatives now consciously fashion responses to the evidence concerning opinion, and they have to think through the rationale behind their responses. Officials' consciousness of the quantified evidence, their sensitivity to the often contradictory nature of the evidence (different wordings of questions on the same subjects will strongly affect how survey respondents answer the questions), and their awareness that they must make *some* choice all factor into how they think about representing their constituents and the public.

The scientific character of the professionally designed and reputable surveys means that they cannot be safely dismissed. Except for Internet surveys (which are mathematically weighted to take account of self-selection) individuals do *not* select themselves for scientific surveys, as they do when they phone the White House or write a letter to the editor or show up at a rally. They instead are selected at random. The myriad differences in respondents' degrees of certainty about their policy views tend to cancel one another out (because the differences are largely random). Survey responses routinely and regularly expose an underlying distribution of policy opinion with a mix of central tendency and dispersion along an opinion spectrum. (Surveys also detect the proportion who are sensible enough to say that they "don't know" or something similar.) The underlying distribution of policy preferences is altogether coherent and, on the merits, quite reasonable, particularly if one is tracing the answers to policy questions that are asked the same way over decades.

Caveats

Should pollsters be middlemen between the people and government? The term "pollster" was invented in 1949 by a political scientist who was unhappy about the rise of polling; he wanted a word that rhymed with the 1946 invention of "huckster" to disparage marketing executives. Pundits have long denounced "government by polling," believing that the public is ill informed. Other analysts think that politicians manipulate the public so that the polls tell the politicians what they want to hear.

Political scientists are less concerned about manipulation. Politicians do have message consultants. But neither political party dominates the country, the airwaves, or the bandwidths. Media bias is regularly discussed on the Left and the Right, a discussion that itself helps to correct bias. Citizens also have an inherent distrust of the media. As for corporate control of the American mind, one could point to the campaign finance case of January 2010, *Citizens United v. Federal Election Commission*. The Supreme Court decided that the principle of free speech required lifting regulatory limits on political advocacy by corporations and unions. They can now directly and independently contribute to political action committees (PACs) that advertise on behalf of political candidates, and those PACs can run their campaign ads when they choose. The case certainly raised the specter of a tidal wave of negative campaign advertising, and some members of Congress and state legislators have found themselves barraged by misleading ads and have thus lost their seats. But close students of the advertising wars in American politics currently doubt that there is an overall bias toward any constituency, group, or party.

The media environment of citizenship has in fact become highly fragmented, with formats for news delivery rapidly evolving and with news consumption increasingly custom-built by citizens to suit their own tastes. National newspapers of record, such as the *New York Times* and the *Washington Post*, have seen their circulations shrink sharply in the past decade. The major broadcast networks long ago ceded their monopoly of the broadcast environment, as cable television and the Internet offer fierce competition. The decentralized structure of communications impedes the manipulation of public opinion.

Additionally, no single political figure can command the attention of the public for very long, with the possible exception of the president. Still, aside from the unique crisis atmosphere that attends a truly grave emergency in national security, presidents cannot—contrary to popular belief—control opinion. In fact, presidential approval ratings never permanently shift after ordinary presidential addresses to the country.

The most basic reason for not worrying about manipulation is that the public has to be paying quite close attention without anything else competing for its attention in order for it to be manipulated in the first place. Yet citizen attention to public affairs is episodic. When the public suddenly does pay close attention to some new aspect of public affairs, when President Bill Clinton was impeached in the House of Representatives and tried in the Senate, for instance, the public also receives a lot of new and conflicting interpretations about the events that suddenly fascinate them.

Consistency between opinion and policy

The bottom line for risk-averse politicians is that they cannot afford to entirely discount the evidence from policy polls. Responses to sensibly phrased questions invariably make too much sense and are too plausible to be sloughed off. They shift in sensible ways in response to major social trends or important new information.

Modern polling thus changes how representatives represent. An additional new standard for representation has emerged besides, for example, earning the trust of one's constituency or, in the case of women's, Latino, Asian American, and African American representation in Congress, providing more of a social mirror in the national legislature. Representatives must now think about matching their decisions about public policy and what public opinion polls tell them that the public wants.

Such change in how representatives represent can be seen in an episode from the Iran-Contra hearings of late spring and summer of 1987. The Iran-Contra hearings were a crucial part of a historic congressional investigation. Mid-level officials in the Reagan administration, based in the White House itself, had covertly and without the president's knowledge sold weapons to the Iranian government in violation of an arms export control act passed in the wake of the Iranian Revolution (the United States had been a major weapons supplier to Iran before the revolution). The funds generated by these sales were then covertly transferred by this secretive circle to a guerrilla insurgency in Nicaragua, known as the Contras, who were fighting the pro-Castro revolutionary government. Yet Congress had forbidden any financial or material support to the Contras.

In televised testimony before Congress, one of the officials, Col. Oliver North (who soon won the admiration of many Americans), ardently defended the illegal programs as sound and necessary.

Col. North was a media sensation: he was plainly patriotic and deeply sincere, yet polls showed consistent and high levels of public opposition to aiding the Contras.

Thus Sen. Warren Rudman (R-New Hampshire) pointed out that public opinion could not be ignored, even if people who really understood policy questions deeply disagreed: "I guess the last thing I want to say to you, Colonel, is that the American people have the constitutional right to be wrong. And what Ronald Reagan thinks or what Oliver North thinks or what I think or what anybody else thinks makes not a whit if the American people say enough."

As a member of Congress, Rudman certainly knew that on a wide range of policy questions he had considerable (and somewhat vexing) freedom in how he represented New Hampshire voters. As he told a scholar, "I would vote thirty-one times some days in the United States Senate. . . . On 99.9 percent of the issues you don't know what your constituency thinks. You know what some people who wrote to you think of you, but those are people who generally feel strongly about the issue." Public opinion on aid to the Contras was different though: via media outlets, the issue was well disseminated and salient. In that circumstance there *was* a clear collective preference, and Sen. Rudman believed that government policy should reflect it.

Just how much correspondence is there between the policies that government produces and what the public wants? Analysts who study policy-making processes have identified and counted agreements over time between the opinion majority for a policy (for example, keeping Medicare fully funded) or a change in policy (for example, increased defense spending) on the one hand, and policy direction and new policies on the other. One study estimated agreement at 64 percent, significantly higher than the chance probability of 50 percent, and variations on the "better than chance" finding have held up in other studies. The relationship is also noticeable in the states:

there is correspondence between the center of public opinion in a state and that state's policy outputs, for example, whether public opinion supports or opposes same-sex marriage.

To be sure, a great deal of policy making is in the hands of experts and advocacy groups, such as national funding for the arts or social science research. Glaring instances of inconsistency are also easy to find. The public overwhelmingly favors a strong federal minimum wage, for instance. Yet the arguments of organized small business and professional economists have blocked its revision to account for inflation, so its real, inflation-adjusted value has fallen sharply. (In response, many states now have living wage laws.) Democrats enacted the health reform of 2010 despite a clear division in public opinion.

Consistency thus varies across time, across policy areas, and across jurisdictions. Some analysts report that it varies according to income level and that the policy views of better-off Americans are generally better represented. Consistency also varies by how much the public thinks about an issue. The more citizens think about an issue the better defined public opinion is about that issue.

Still, the last word here goes to figures such as George Gallup, one of the pioneers of private-sector polling. Gallup ended the career of the once-famous *Literary Digest*, a magazine that used vast mail surveys to predict the outcome of presidential elections. On the basis of a 23 percent response rate to a 10 million–postcard survey, the magazine confidently predicted that Alf Landon, the Republican governor of Kansas, would win 57 percent of the popular vote in the 1936 presidential election, defeating the incumbent president Franklin D. Roosevelt. Gallup, an advertising executive, had set up his own private polling operation in Princeton, New Jersey, and boldly announced that the *Digest* was sure to be wrong. Gallup fielded a large team of in-person interviewers—and he thought that he had a more representative sample of opinion. Gallup was right; the *Digest* was wrong. The real landslide was 62 percent for Roosevelt.

7. George Gallup at the University of Iowa in the 1920s. A decade later, Gallup helped to develop the survey research that today provides a way to assess whether government officials and public policy are in accord with public opinion.

Gallup admired a nineteenth-century British democratic theorist, Lord James Bryce, who speculated that a new and better "stage" in democracy might be reached "if the will of the majority were to become ascertainable at all times." Bryce wondered, though, if such "machinery for weighing or measuring the popular will from week to week or month to month" could actually be invented. Gallup believed that his polling advances did just that: they allowed the voice of the public to be heard clearly and continuously. His surveys represented the machinery that would realize a new phase in the development of American democracy.

Gallup's own machinery was imperfect, particularly in the way he biased his samples to represent the electorate, not the public, and this meant that he grossly under-sampled African Americans. He later famously predicted Thomas Dewey's non-victory over President Harry Truman in the 1948 presidential election because he stopped polling too far in advance of

Election Day. Gallup and his fellow pioneers in polling (such as Archibald Crossley and Elmo Roper) nonetheless paved a new way for elected officials to represent the public. They founded an extra-constitutional context for political representation that has steadily grown in importance.

Chapter 8
Political parties and democratic choice

The basic political dualism in the United States—of constitutional and extra-constitutional institutions connected to each other—emerged earlier than most Americans realize. George Washington's 1796 Farewell Address represents a reaction to that dualism's embryonic appearance. Upon voluntarily stepping down after two terms as president, Washington urged his fellow Founders and citizens to unite behind making the American experiment work. Washington abhorred the division among those who made and ratified the Constitution of 1787. Fearing that elite factions would ruin the Constitution, he pictured political parties as a serious danger: "Let me . . . warn you in the most solemn manner against the baneful effects of the spirit of party. . . . It exists under different shapes in all governments, more or less stifled, controlled, or repressed; but, in those of the popular form, it is seen in its greatest rankness, and is truly their worst enemy."

Washington's warning hardly mattered. The Federalists, the once-cohesive coalition of notables who devised and implemented the Constitution of 1787, had already split apart into two "proto-parties": the Federalists, led by Alexander Hamilton and

Washington's successor, John Adams, and the Republicans, soon to be *National* Republicans as their party grew (and soon after that it was the Democratic-Republicans, the precursor of today's Democratic party). This opposing party was led by Thomas Jefferson, who became Adams's vice president, and by James Madison.

Madison had busied himself with party-building during the Washington and Adams administrations, developing a network of partisan newspapers for his side. This was a different Madison than the figure who defended the Constitution in the *Federalist* (a collection of opinion pieces that is now considered an authoritative commentary on the various elements of the Constitution of 1787). In the *Federalist* Madison and his co-authors, John Jay and Alexander Hamilton, portrayed the intricacy of constitutional design as one of the Constitution's sturdiest safeguards. But Alexander Hamilton's energy as Secretary of the Treasury startled Madison. He worried that the Constitution was vulnerable to centralization.

By building a political party to protest Hamilton's program for strengthening the federal government, Madison hit on an effective formula that stabilized the Constitution. A competitive party system promoted popular appreciation of the Constitution's intricate, complicated, checking-and-balancing politics. Politicians acquired a vested interest in perpetuating its institutions. In contending for office they could regularly discuss the various constitutional powers and in so doing broadly educate the citizenry. Bringing voters into the conversation would also develop the state and local governments, for parties would be organized not only bottom down, from Congress, but also bottom up, thus building federalism.

George Washington's alternative to Madison's party-building was virtuous statesmanship. But as the nineteenth century beckoned, the task of making the new Constitution work fell not to patrician guardians but to political parties. The new national government took shape through and alongside party conflict and growing participation.

How political parties shaped citizenship

Early-nineteenth-century state legislatures took the lead in expanding the suffrage and in making the vote for president a popular vote. Parties created slates for presidential electors. Article 2, section 1 of the Constitution specified procedures for indirectly electing the president. It allocated "electors" of the president to each state. That number of electors equaled the sum of the number of senators for each state (two) and the number of representatives for each state (in turn, a number determined by a state's population, which is revealed by the U.S. Census every ten years.) Initially the states varied in how they provided for the selection of these electors. In many states the legislature chose the electors, but between 1800 and 1824 the states permitting a popular vote for presidential electors grew from five out of sixteen to eighteen out of twenty-four. In the process, the political parties broadened their electoral foundations.

By the early 1820s, though, the party-building process faltered as the Federalists, George Washington's own party, collapsed. They opposed the War of 1812 and thus seemed deeply unpatriotic. Ambitious politicians did not want to ruin their careers by affiliating with it. The United States now had one dominant party—the Democratic-Republican party.

Party factionalism set in motion the next party-building phase. Democratic-Republican blocs fielded a total of four presidential candidates in 1824. At this point another suffrage expansion occurred—this time in the wake of the presidential election's determination by the House of Representatives. The Constitution provided that each state would vote as a unit in the House of Representatives if the regular presidential election did not produce a winner who took a simple majority of the presidential electors. Because the 1824 election did not produce such a winner, the House proceeded to vote. By today's standards it should have chosen the apparent winner. This was Andrew Jackson, America's preeminent war hero, who led the United States to victory against British forces at the Battle of New Orleans in January 1815. But the House instead chose John Quincy Adams, even though Adams's share of the popular vote and his share of the electoral vote were both smaller than Jackson's.

Capitalizing on popular outrage over the House's selection of Adams, Andrew Jackson mounted a second campaign for the presidency from his home state of Tennessee. His renewed quest for the presidency gathered steam through state legislative endorsements, conventions, and public meetings, all culminating in his election in 1828. Participation soared: only about 366,000 men voted in 1824, but about 1,149,000 voted four years later. Jackson and his party divided the country, however, and by 1840 his handpicked successor, Martin Van Buren, faced fierce competition from a new party, the Whigs. Voter participation had grown, and the party system regained its competitiveness.

Several defining elements of party competition thus emerged between Washington's Farewell Address and 1840: vigorous competition, contestation over principles and visions of where the country should go as the parties began to write and publicize platforms, and lively popular involvement in politics. Only white adult males could vote, and their acquisition of voting rights was accompanied by the deliberate exclusion of women and free African Americans. The new white male populism also fueled conquest and expansion aimed at Mexico and Native Americans. Still, the new party politics deeply engaged those who were eligible to vote. Party politics provided what popular, outdoor entertainment there was. Campaigns featured torchlight parades in villages, towns, and cities, uniformed men and boys waving banners and wearing buttons and ribbons, floats designed by ladies' auxiliaries, and mass rallies to attend public orations. Turnout among the new republic of white, male eligible voters was very high, and the pool of such eligible voters continually expanded from immigration, incorporation of new states, and population growth.

New parties could form to inject new issues into the discussion, since all they had to do was to print the ballots (unlike today, when they must gather enough signatures of support to convince state governments to add them to the ballots printed by the states). The Republican party began, in fact, as a third party devoted to stopping the spread of slavery. After the Civil War, issue-based parties continued to emerge well into the 1890s, raising popular concerns about (among other matters) monetary policy (then directly controlled by Congress), and prohibition and temperance.

The new mass democratic republic grew and expanded after the Civil War. Reconstruction and Republican party-building in the South brought in nearly a million former slaves as first-class voters. Black voting in the South was immensely controversial, but it persisted for several decades, into the 1890s.

In 1884 Whitman lauded that year's election day—though it is not an election that today we consider especially noteworthy.

> If I should need to name, O Western World!
>   your powerfulest scene to-day,
> 'Twould not be you, Niagara—nor you, ye
>   limitless prairies—nor your huge
>   rifts of canyons, Colorado,
> . . .
> I'd name—*the still small voice* preparing—
>   America's choosing day,

> (The heart of it not in the chosen—the act
>   itself the main, the quadrennial
>   choosing,)
> . . .
> The final ballot-shower from East to West—
>   the paradox and conflict,
> The countless snow-flakes falling—(a sword-
>   less conflict . . .

That a great poet sang to electoral democracy underscores the sheer novelty of mass voting and popular choice in the New World.

Transfer of power

In addition to issues, choice and involvement in public affairs for millions of ordinary people political parties also taught both elites and voters valuable lessons about *transfer of power*. The 1800 election provided the first occasion for this lesson.

8. The political cartoonist Thomas Nast visualized the elephant as the symbol of the Republican Party with this 1874 cartoon and several others that he published around that time. The party today incorporates the elephant into its campaign websites and paraphernalia.

That election featured a deep constitutional crisis. When the votes of the presidential electors were tallied, a tie emerged between the opposition presidential candidate, Thomas Jefferson, and his vice presidential running mate, Aaron Burr. (Only later, with the Twelfth Amendment that was ratified in 1804, did the electors cast separate ballots for president and vice president.) To whom would presidential power be transferred? The House now chose the president, as specified by the Constitution. Because Federalists controlled the House, the Federalists were tempted to award the election to their favored candidate, Aaron Burr, thus depriving their avowed foe, Thomas Jefferson, of victory. Civil war threatened as the state militias of Virginia and Pennsylvania assembled to prevent Burr's installation. George Washington's worst fears might well have been realized. But after thirty-six ballots, and in response to Alexander Hamilton's pressure on his fellow Federalists to give way, the House elected Thomas Jefferson as president.

America's fledgling parties thus embraced the principle that upon the governing coalition's electoral defeat, in presidential or other national elections, there must be a peaceful transfer of power to the victorious opposition—since opposition was legitimate. This vital practice even played a role during the Civil War, in connection with the presidential election of 1864. Supporters of Lincoln and pro–Civil War Democrats formed the Republican Union Party; the Democrats put forth a Union Civil War general as their presidential nominee. They hoped that they could force Abraham Lincoln from the White House and broker a peace with the South. Had Lincoln lost there is little doubt that he would have stepped aside.

The Electoral College

Another result of the 1800 election crisis was the Twelfth Amendment to the Constitution. Proposed in December 1803 and ratified by June 1804, in time for the new election, it required presidential electors to vote separately for president and vice president, foreclosing a replay of something like the Jefferson-Burr tie that threw the 1800 election into the House. The new amendment constitutionalized party tickets—that is, presidential candidates campaigning with a vice-presidential running mate.

Over the next several decades after passage of the Twelfth Amendment, the parties developed the Electoral College more or less as we know it today. Voters grasped that they were indirectly voting for their own party notables – the presidential electors for a state whose number equaled the state's number of U.S. House representatives and its two U.S. Senators. "The people" thus chose for president and vice-president, if at one remove. They were visually reminded of the indirection, both during the campaign and on election day itself, when they asked for ballots with clearly marked elector slates. But voters also understood that the indirect choice was ultimately popular.

In return, the parties gained greater finality for the presidential election, so long as the popular vote simultaneously generated a winner in the Electoral College. The Constitution did not, it is worth remembering, refer by name to an Electoral College. The Constitution and the Twelfth Amendment described only a system of indirect voting for the president in state capitals by electors equal to the number of senators and U.S. House members for that state. The term "Electoral College" was first formalized in an 1845 federal statute (still in the U.S. Code) that established the national election date for presidential voting, the first Tuesday after the first Monday in November, and which referred to a "College of Electors." This change weighted the outcome of the presidential vote in the sense that the popular vote winner (and the running mate) acquired the weight of the Constitution's authority for their popular victory.

Today the voters in forty-eight states and the District of Columbia (the exceptions are Maine and Nebraska) decide a winner-take-all plurality victory for an invisible slate comprising real people who are chosen carefully by the formal party organization of each state. Maine, since 1972, and Nebraska, since 1996, use a "congressional district method," in which congressional districts separately award their votes even as the statewide winner collects the two "Senate" votes; so far the statewide winner has won all of the votes in these states without splits.

In all states, the size of each party's slate equals the size of the total congressional delegation. This is why the sparsely populated states have three votes in the Electoral College. Members of the winning slate later meet, formally, in December, in their state's capital, to directly cast their votes for the presidential candidate to whom they are pledged (informally, as it happens, in twenty states) to vote. These electors are agents of a principal—the coalition of voters who won the plurality or majority for the winning ticket in that state. Then, from the state capital, the actual physical votes are sent to the archivist of the United States and to the president pro tem of the U.S. Senate to be opened and openly counted in early January, at which time there is formally a new president. This ancient process punctuates and finalizes the popular vote.

Modern misgivings

Voters today no longer see the names of the electors in the voting booth, and this probably explains why the Electoral College today mystifies and irritates so many citizens. Contemporary presidential elections inspire hand-wringing in civics classes about the faithless elector problem, that is, the possibility of an elector ignoring the instruction from the ballots (a great rarity that has never actually made a difference). Another concern is the fear that the Electoral College can systematically favor one party over the other. For example, one party can become so strong in a region that its candidate always has an edge going into the election season.

Many people find it odd that voters in small, sparsely populated states seem to have more "voting power" than voters in large, densely populated states. As an example, about 533,000 eligible voters in North Dakota get three electoral votes, or one elector per 177,666 voters, roughly, while California's much larger electorate of about 23.6 million eligible voters gets fifty-five electoral votes, or one for about every 429,455 voters. Others point out that the reverse seems to be the case, since presidential candidates seldom visit small states during the general election. The votes that count are those that are competed for. Yet others, following this logic, point out that the country is now sorted into "battleground" states, where voters are intensively canvassed, and "spectator" states, where voters are left alone, creating a two-tiered system for participation that depresses citizen engagement with politics. This particular objection has fueled the National Popular Vote Initiative, an idea for an interstate compact first introduced in February 2006 in the Illinois legislature and has been joined since then by several states. The idea is that a state's electoral votes go automatically to the winner of the national popular vote regardless of the vote balance in the state itself. When enough states have signed on to the plan to reach the Electoral College's 270-vote majority threshold the compact would, presumably, go into effect.

Political scientists, however, have not found large, persistent biases in the Electoral College. One scholar has compared the Democratic share of the national popular vote and the Democratic vote share in the median Electoral College "unit" (since the District of Columbia gets three votes.) The difference between these two vote shares has ranged from +1.8 for 1948 (Democratic national vote share higher that year than vote share in median Electoral College unit) to –.1 for 2004, with no average difference between 1948 and 2008.

Managing and adapting the legacy

A more serious problem with the Electoral College—and it is an enduring difficulty—is that, paradoxically, it can fail to finalize an election. The operation of the Electoral College, when it interacts either with fierce or irregular contention in a key state or states or with uncertain vote counting by state and local election administrators, can actually undercut the vital finality and legitimacy that a presidential election requires. A particularly lengthy such crisis occurred in the disputed election of 1876. The Republican candidate, Rutherford B. Hayes, appeared to win the Electoral College while the Democratic candidate, Samuel Tilden, won the popular vote. Democrats contended, however, that Hayes's margin in the Electoral College was based on fraud in three southern states, and Republicans contended that Tilden's supposed victories in these same southern states depended on election day violence against Republicans, particularly African American voters. A special electoral commission settled the crisis on the eve of the inauguration. Over the next decade Congress discussed how to settle such disputes, and it eventually produced a statutory framework, still on the books, for resolving disputed elections, the Electoral Count Act of 1887.

Most recently, of course, there was the standoff of 2000 when the allocation of the state of Florida's votes in the Electoral College ended up in the Florida courts. The secretary of state of Florida initially awarded the state's votes to George W. Bush, the Republican. She also happened to have a formal role in the Bush presidential campaign in Florida. Because her award depended on a few hundred hotly disputed votes, Bush's opponent, the Democrat Al Gore, persuaded the Florida Supreme Court to order a recount of the vote. The two sides eventually turned to the Supreme Court and effectively invited it to choose the winner. The U.S. Supreme Court, which at the time consisted of five conservatives and four liberals, halted the vote recount that the Florida Supreme Court had ordered and held that the recount process established by that court could not treat all of the state's voters equally, as required by the Fourteenth Amendment to the Constitution. As a result, the original certification of George W. Bush as the winner in Florida by the secretary of state was left standing—and George W. Bush became the forty-third president of the United States.

The rise of party politics in the nineteenth century promoted popular discussion of the issues of the day and simultaneously helped build the Constitution. Politicians wanted to perpetuate the institutions to which they were elected. Their careerism and ambition were attached to the interests of the offices that they held. Party politicians also explained to voters what the constitutional institutions did—the presidency, Congress, the Supreme Court, the governorships, and the state legislatures. Finally, through developing the Electoral College and making it work most of the time, the parties mutually institutionalized and bequeathed a way to select America's chief executive. Should the Electoral College break down again as dramatically as it did in 1876 and 2000, though, America's political parties will hear calls for reconstructing it on a new basis—or for improving how state and local elections officials count votes. As in the past, the political parties will preside over a national conversation about establishing the right institutional connections between democratic voting and constitutional procedures.

Chapter 9
The partisan revival

Strong partisan and ideological differences now define contemporary American politics, but these are recent developments. From the late 1960s into the 1990s many citizens split their votes between Democrats and Republicans. During a presidential election year a white southerner might support a Democrat running for governor of her state even as she voted for the Republican presidential candidate. In House and Senate elections many voters supported candidates on the basis of their personal appeal—the so-called personal vote. Landslides were fairly common in presidential elections, suggesting that many voters could easily put aside their attachments to their parties in the excitement of a campaign. In three of those presidential elections, the winners garnered around 60 percent of the popular vote. In 1964 the incumbent president Lyndon Johnson won reelection with 61 percent of the popular vote; in 1972 the incumbent Richard Nixon was reelected with just over 60 percent; and in 1984 the incumbent Ronald Reagan was reelected with about 59 percent.

More recent presidential elections have been cliff-hangers. The 2000, 2004, 2008, and 2012 presidential elections were hard fought. Ideological separation among politicians is another feature of contemporary party politics. Technical measures of ideological polarization between Left and Right in Congress show that legislators have grown farther apart since the late 1970s, and voters have noticed this change. Nearly three of five voters see the Democratic party as liberal even as they see the Republican party as conservative. More than 80 percent of Republicans see Democrats as liberal, while 61 percent of Democrats see the Republicans as conservative.

Americans have in fact entered what might be called a second party period. Political historians devised the term "party period" for the nineteenth-century heyday of American political parties, from roughly 1840 to 1900. During these decades, political parties and electoral politics mattered viscerally to voters. To say that the United States is in a second party period captures the increased party loyalty among voters and their noticeable movement into opposing ideological camps. The ambition and careerism of politicians have always made electoral and party politics highly competitive. But the extent to which the voters really cared about parties, elections, and the issues of the day has varied, and the United States is now in an era of particularly strong partisan passions.

Many pundits remark on the "independent" swing voters, yet their role is exaggerated. When surveys follow up with questions about whether voters "lean" toward a major party or are "closer" to it, they show that the number of "strict independents," so to speak, is small, about 10 to 11 percent of all voters, possibly fewer.

Indeed, partisan voters are increasingly loyal to their party candidates. The Republican president Ronald Reagan won support from many Democrats in 1980 and 1984—hence the term "Reagan Democrats." But exit polls (surveys of voters after they have just left a polling area) in 2008 showed that about 89 percent of Democrats voted for Barack Obama and about 89 percent of Republican voters voted for John McCain.

As for voters, the number of people who call themselves "moderate, middle of the road" has declined: 27 percent in

1972 and 22 percent in 2008. There has also been gradual sorting to the Left and the Right since 1972. The percentage who say they "haven't thought" about where to put themselves in a scale ranging from "extremely liberal" to "extremely conservative" has dropped from a high of 36 percent in 1980 to 25 percent in 2008. As the "moderate" and "haven't thought" percentages dropped, voters necessarily shifted themselves away from the center.

Self-identified conservatives among voters have always outnumbered self-identified liberals—sometimes by wide margins as in 1994. The trend in conservative identification has been about a six-point increase, from 26 percent in 1972 to 32 percent in 2008. But the trend on the liberal side is nearly as large, four points, from 18 percent in 1972 to 22 percent by 2008.

Thus ideology and partisanship increasingly coincide. Find a Republican, and you have probably also found a conservative on the issues (and vice versa). Only 4 percent of Republicans call themselves liberal; just 16 percent of Republicans call themselves moderates. About 12 percent of Democrats call themselves conservative, and 22 percent of Democrats think of themselves as moderate. African Americans, who are traditionally very strong Democrats, tend to be more culturally conservative than white liberals. There are more self-identified Democrats than Republicans, so the Democratic party is more ideologically heterogeneous. But voters who think of themselves as liberals and who take liberal stances on issues such as abortion, gay rights, or national reform of health insurance, are overwhelmingly Democrats.

Besides ideological sorting, partisan rancor and suspicion have grown. Television, radio, cable TV, and blogs and Internet publications are more one-sided. During the first party period of the nineteenth century this was also true; newspapers were highly partisan and slanted.

Charges of election fraud were frequent, precisely because the parties were so competitive, which meant that elections were close. In an echo of nineteenth-century suspicions, election administration has again become politicized. Many Democrats noticed that the chief election officials of key battleground states—Florida (2000) and Ohio (2004)—also were active in the Republican presidential campaigns. Democrats have also come to think that Republicans prefer to keep minority voters away from the polls. Saying that they wish to prevent voter fraud, Republicans have promoted legislation that requires voters to show some form of official identification at the polls. But many Democrats say that "voter ID" (as this sort of legislation is called) is really about making it harder for minority voters to vote. Many Republicans, for their part, believe that Democrats work with voter registration groups in ways that skirt legality.

Turnout has also increased. Turnout is a ratio—it can be the number who voted relative to number of people legally eligible to vote, or it can be the number who voted relative to the voting-age population. The two populations are not the same, due to both the influx of legal and undocumented immigrants and the increased incarceration of adult males, which has increased the population of citizens disenfranchised by felony convictions. Currently there are about 217 million people eligible to vote in the United States, but the voting age population is about 236 million. The first version of turnout, based on those who are eligible to vote, usefully captures the degree to which party and electoral politics engage citizens. Turnout among citizens eligible to vote in presidential elections— about 62 percent nationally—has nearly returned to the national level that it had in 1960. Among the states, turnout ranges from 49 percent in Hawaii to 78 percent in Minnesota.

Besides the increased turnout, there has also been a jump in the extent to which voters try to influence how others vote—another sign of growing mass interest in politics. The American National Election Studies (operated by the University of Michigan) biennially asks, "During the campaign, did you talk to any people and try to show them why they should vote for or against one of the parties or candidates?" In 1990, the percentage answering yes was 17 percent; in 2008 it was 28 points higher at 45 percent.

Then and now

In short, if a nineteenth-century voter traveled through time to the present, he might find himself in a familiar political context. Yet institutionally the new party period differs from the nineteenth-century party period in ways that this time-traveling voter would also quickly remark.

Temporary—but large and movement-style—third parties were regular features of the 1840–1900 party period. At one time state and local parties directly and informally ran elections: they printed ballots (subject to basic requirements set by state legislatures), and they conducted the vote counting. Third (and fourth) parties easily formed: their campaign workers simply showed up with their ballots at the polls.

Today the chances of third-party success are lower—much lower. Many states require that voters (the exact numbers vary across states) petition for placement of a third party on the state-produced ballot. Third-party activists cannot just show up with valid ballots on election day at the polls. Instead, the state and local governments register voters, devise the ballots, distribute and manage polling stations, acquire and maintain voting machines, and count the votes. The electoral process legally and administratively advantages the major parties.

Party politics used to happen outdoors—much more than it does today. The party-organized parades, rallies, encampments, and barbeques of the nineteenth century are now uncommon. Social movements, not parties, today do more to organize "liberal" or "conservative" public rallies at, say, the National Mall in Washington, D.C.

Candidate selection and recruitment also differ. Toward the end of the first party period, many state parties shifted from the party nominating convention to the more formal mechanism of the party primary election. Party politicians preferred the shift because it rewarded individual political skills in appealing to voters. During the twentieth century, the primary system spread among the states. Parties now largely select their presidential nominees over several months of sequential elections, as intraparty presidential candidates try to force their rivals out and also to build a majority of convention delegates (according to quadrennially evolving rules decided by national and state organizations). The winning candidate saves the choice of the vice presidential nominee for the convention or just before it in order to unify the party and focus public attention. Highly motivated partisans thus experience nominations as long marches that take almost a year.

Presidential candidates did not personally campaign during the first party period, although congressional candidates did. Patronage workers—public employees whose jobs depend on an informal agreement that they knock on doors for the party—contacted voters. For much of the first party period such workers came, in fact, from the U.S. customs houses, naval shipyards, and the post office. State and local parties used state and local public employees whenever possible.

Campaigning is now personalized and professionalized. Electioneering by public employees has effectively disappeared in most of the country. Candidates instead hurtle through sixteen- to twenty-hour days of retail, "vote-for-me" politicking, often showing up at events organized by others. A magazine reporter covering a candidate for the U.S. Senate in 2010 noted that the candidate's "approach to campaigning falls somewhere between tireless and maniacal. When the Independence Day parade got started, he was determined to shake as many hands as possible, so he took off on a trot."

To help plan and manage such strenuous activity, and also to make sure that they do not blunder from fatigue, candidates for hotly contested races rely on hired campaign professionals. These professionals include media consultants who produce television or radio ads and, increasingly, interactive websites. Presidential, gubernatorial, and senatorial campaigns employ pollsters who let the consultants know whether their coaching, message management, and advice are working.

Candidates also depend on volunteers who are psychologically committed to a candidate or a party or both. After work and on weekends at campaign offices, volunteers make phone calls, get in cars to distribute lawn signs, knock on doors to distribute campaign literature, stand at traffic stops with campaign placards, and the like. Though only about 3 percent of the public reports such volunteering during national election years, that is still a very large number of volunteers.

Since 1990 the percentage of the public that has been contacted by campaigns from either major party has grown by more than 100 percent. Almost everyone (about 86 percent) is exposed to campaign advertising or political reporting on television during national election years. Increasingly, too, citizens follow national campaigns on the Internet.

In addition to campaign reporting and television advertising, the introduction of television facilitated the innovation of formal debates between primary and general election presidential (and increasingly gubernatorial and senatorial) candidates. Formal election debates predated the partisan renaissance by a generation. But they survive today and have become fixtures because they fit with the new, sharper party competition.

Television ownership spread rapidly among American households between 1956 and 1960. The Democratic presidential candidate and Illinois senator Adlai Stevenson, working with a visionary young aide, Newton Minow, promoted the idea that television would permit great issues debates. Illinois, not coincidentally, had been the site of the Lincoln-Douglas Debates in the senatorial race of 1858. In 1960, just after the centennial of the Lincoln-Douglas Debates, these ideas promoted by Stevenson and Minow came to early fruition in a series of four debates between John F. Kennedy and Richard Nixon. After a hiatus, the 1976 Democratic nominee, former Georgia governor Jimmy Carter, was challenged by President Gerald Ford on national television "to go before the American People and debate the real issues face to face." Since 1976 every presidential election has featured formal debates between the presidential candidates, first under the sponsorship of the League of Women Voters and then under the auspices of the federal Commission on Presidential Debates, which has organized debates since 1988.

Competitive party politics and political polarization inevitably entail accusation and counterattack during campaigns. This prominent feature of competitive elections has prompted newspapers and nonprofit websites to publish campaign ad "fact checks." Negativity was just as great, however, during the first party period: a highly decentralized and openly partisan press reeked with vitriol. The difference is that voters today experience campaign negativity in their homes, while they are watching television for entertainment or in bars and at their health clubs. Negativity is invasive today in a way not possible in the nineteenth century. Yet political scientists have come to suspect that the point-counterpoint of contrasting ads is informative, and survey evidence shows that voters themselves recognize that.

The new party period's competitiveness also strongly influences the role of money in elections. Money per se is not driving politics and policy. Instead, the fury of political competition draws money in. American campaign finance is deeply rooted in the relentless biennial frequency of national elections. Additionally, the length and two-stage nature of the many bids for office—first primaries and then general elections—contribute to the cost of elections in the United States.

There are "big donors." But big donors are intensely ideological. Instead of investing in specific policy outcomes, say a tax break for their company, they are investing in different visions of what the right approach to policy should be, such as reducing the size of government overall. Rich donors also offset each other. Wealthy liberals are a major source of funding for the Democratic party; similarly, wealthy conservatives give to the Republicans. And corporate money flowing to the Republican party is significantly offset by labor union money going to the Democratic party. Finally, both parties rely on broad small-donor bases.

Government regulation and reporting of campaign finance also distinguish the first party period from the current party period. During the first party period money was also very important—but *how* the parties raised money was not publicly reported nor available to researchers and reporters. The 1972 Federal Election Campaign Act established the current system of reporting. In 1974 an amendment to that act established the Federal Election Commission that collects and disseminates detailed information about campaign finance and regulations. This national system forms just one part of campaign finance regulation. The National Conference of State Legislatures and the Campaign Finance Institute websites provide links to all of the state campaign finance laws and agencies.

Another contrast between present and past is coordination between advocacy groups and political parties around initiatives and referenda. Between 1898 (in South Dakota) and 1918 (Massachusetts), twenty-two states adopted the device (imported from Switzerland) of sending popular, bottom-up instructions to legislators via the ballot. Oregon, California,

Colorado, North Dakota, Arizona, and Washington today use the ballot initiative—a legislative proposal that voters directly decide. It has neither an inherent populist or conservative tilt; some ballot initiatives have mandated environmental cleanups, others have banned same-sex marriage and limited government spending. Either way, the initiative allows liberal and conservative groups affiliated with the parties to influence a state's agenda, that is, what its representative institutions consider in addition to nondiscretionary items, such as budgeting. When state initiatives capture national attention, as California's have with tax and immigration policies, organized groups in one state can influence the entire country.

Voting today is secret—and this would instantly strike a visitor from the nineteenth century. In the first period, voting by adult men was public in the sense that one asked for the party-printed ballot as he entered the booth or room for voting, so he therefore did not have to be literate to vote. Election day disturbances were also common, and federal marshals in many cities kept public order. Sometimes campaigns became militarized, particularly in the South during Reconstruction, and featured irregular troops of armed men parading the countryside as election day grew near. Today voting is a secluded, peaceful act that demands literacy.

Moreover, election day has begun to fade as a collective experience. In many jurisdictions, election day has given way to an election period because early voting is increasingly allowed. Voting in person now coexists with voting by mail either through absentee balloting (for college students, travelers, and so forth) or balloting from overseas (for members of the military). In Oregon, all voting is done by mail. About a third of all voters in the United States vote before election day. If Walt Whitman were alive today he would have to think twice about penning an ode to election day as a simultaneous national democratic experience, as he did in 1884.

9. A Minneapolis voter, Ira Stafford, fills out his ballot at a crowded polling place in 2008. Although early and absentee voting have increased, most Americans still vote in person on election day.

Knowledge of "who won" spreads much more quickly than it did in the nineteenth century. The presidential election winner is usually known by survey researchers who work for the major television networks. When they know for certain who won it is because they took accurate representative samples from voters as they left the polls. The public thus usually learns who won the presidency either after citizens eat dinner on election day or the next morning when they wake up, and they learn the news from the privately run media, courtesy of social science techniques.

Partisan renewal and democratic renewal

The first and second party periods differ not only in how candidates and parties contest elections but also on another vital dimension: whom they bring in and whom they keep out. American party and electoral politics today are generally far more legally inclusive than during the first party period and, for that matter, during much of the twentieth century. The two major parties today mobilize voters at a lower rate—turnout among those who are legally eligible to vote (as defined by state statutes and constitutions under article 1, section 4 of the Constitution) was about twenty percentage points higher during the first party period. Poorer and poorly educated voters are today less mobilized than other voters. In many elections there are marked class and racial biases in turnout.

Immigrants are also not eligible to vote. The backlash to the sharp increase in the late twentieth century of both the legal and undocumented immigrant populations make any return to non-citizen voting, nineteenth-century style, extremely unlikely for now. A byproduct of more people being sent to jail than ever before is more felon disenfranchisement than ever before. Voters in Puerto Rico (which has a special constitutional affiliation with the United States) and in such dependencies as Guam, the Marianas, Samoa, and the Virgin Islands do not have the civic status of continental voters—unless they establish residency in one of the fifty states. Voters in the District of Columbia do not enjoy full and equal congressional representation.

But such disturbing contemporary exclusions—as offensive as they rightly are to many observers of American politics—look less odious in historical perspective. The first party period ended with suffrage restriction. Complete African American disenfranchisement in the defunct Confederacy; the end of non-citizen voting, which had earlier aided immigrant assimilation; and formal restriction of immigration by the mid-1920s all coincided. There were significant contrasts, of course: the constitutional establishment of female suffrage in 1920, and four years later there was the symbolic statutory creation of Native American suffrage. But neither of these changes altered who did the politicking. By the early twentieth century white adult males were again at the center of American politics, just as they were for much of the nineteenth century.

Today, though, the partisan revival is rebuilding the American nation. The black suffrage amendments (the Fourteenth and Fifteenth Amendments, ratified by three-quarters of the states in 1868 and 1870); the female suffrage amendment (the Nineteenth Amendment, ratified in 1920); yet another amendment intended to strengthen black voting rights (the Twenty-fourth Amendment, abolishing the poll tax, ratified in 1964);and the Twenty-sixth Amendment, which lowered the voting age from twenty-one to eighteen (ratified in 1971) have all finally met much (though hardly all) of their collective potential.

Thanks to the black voting rights struggles that led to the Voting Rights Act of 1965, and to a quieter (but no less consequential) post-1965 struggle in the courts to implement the act, the electoral process has opened up not only to African Americans and to Afro-Caribbeans in Boston, Miami, and New York. It has also pulled in Asian and Native Americans. Native American voters face intimidation in some states, such as South Dakota, but voting rights lawyers and Native American activists are fighting back. Latino voting and office holding have surged in the Southwest and California and in large cities such as Boston, Chicago, Miami, and New York. Voting procedures for members of the armed forces deployed overseas have been regularized and strengthened as well.

Political parties and the elective offices that they populate are today much more diverse—not diverse enough but certainly far more than before. Except for the Reconstruction period, when African American men served in the U.S. House and Senate and in state legislatures and local governments in the South, party and government were long occupied almost entirely by white males. But the long civil rights struggles of the twentieth century eventually brought African Americans and Latinos into the halls of Congress and state legislatures—and into the White House, with the historic election of Barack Obama in 2008. Today one of the Supreme Court justices, Sonia Sotomayor, is Puerto Rican.

The rights struggles of the 1960s and 1970s also widened the impact of women's political activism. All through American political history women have been deeply involved in public affairs; what has changed is the extent of office holding. Thus by 2008 former First Lady and U.S. Senator Hillary Clinton nearly won the Democratic presidential nomination, and the governor of Alaska, Sarah Palin, was the vice-presidential running mate for the Republican presidential candidate, Senator John McCain. The civil rights movement and women's political activism have facilitated, as well, the entrance of lesbians and gays into electoral politics. Gay and lesbian members of state legislatures and Congress form part of a growing mainstream presence for gays and lesbians.

The greater inclusiveness of party and electoral politics has a religious dimension as well, and this too has reshaped office holding. During the first party period Protestantism permeated politics. Evangelical Protestantism is today a major force, particularly in Republican politics, yet the Republican presidential candidate in 2012, Mitt Romney, was extremely active in Mormonism during his entire adult life. During the first party period, in contrast, Mormons were national pariahs. And in a development that would have been unthinkable in the nineteenth century but that today seems perfectly normal, the Supreme Court is composed mostly of Roman Catholics and Jews. Congress today has more Jews serving in it than have ever served in that assembly.

For most of American political history, party and electoral politics was largely (though never entirely) the business of Protestant white adult, apparently heterosexual males. In contrast, today's party and electoral politics, and their impact on who holds public office, reflect American society to a greater degree than ever before.

Chapter 10
Politics in the new Gilded Age

Americans live in a new Gilded Age, a term that denotes an era of immensely unequal riches. The American writer Mark Twain and a Hartford, Connecticut, journalist, Charles Dudley Warner, first coined the expression in 1873 when they published *The Gilded Age: A Tale of Today*, a novel that mocked the way Americans pursued great wealth. During the late 1890s—when the United States was well into its first Gilded Age—political scientists and sociologists debated the merits of what they called the "concentration of wealth." Today a similar debate grips the American social sciences as political scientists, economists, and sociologists puzzle over a profound change in the extent of income inequality.

The debate over unequal riches has migrated into party politics. Democratic politicians take stronger positions against income inequality than most Republicans. Democrats perceive themselves as the party of ordinary people. Surveys show that voters generally share that perception, despite Republican politicians often scolding Democrats for being elitist and out of touch with American values. The Democratic party pushes—even if it does not consistently deliver—for good jobs, low unemployment, and increasing wages for everyone who wants to work. Finally, Democrats affiliate with organized labor—and trade unions are passionate about economic justice. Although the Democratic party is hardly a labor party, it is historically the party of organized labor.

Republicans, in contrast, emphasize how smaller government, less regulation, employers' freedom to hire and fire, and governmental encouragement of the private sector will lift fortunes for all. While Republicans' actions often contradict their stated laissez-faire approach to the private sector (it was a Republican administration that bailed out large banks in crisis in the fall of 2008), it is nonetheless their first principle. They are also more likely than Democrats to fret that making an issue of inequality perversely stigmatizes individual effort and success. In a January 2012 television interview, Matt Lauer of NBC asked Mitt Romney, the Republican presidential candidate, "Are there no fair questions about the distribution of wealth without it being seen as envy?" Romney replied that such discussion should occur in "quiet rooms" but not in presidential campaigns. Denouncing President Obama, Romney said, "The president has made it part of his campaign rally. Everywhere he goes we hear him talking about millionaires and billionaires and executives and Wall Street. It's a very envy-oriented, attack-oriented approach."

An issue here to stay

"Millionaires and billionaires and executives and Wall Street" will probably face criticism for many years. Thanks to award-winning economic research, we know that in the late 1970s those at the very top of the income scale began to achieve steady increases in both income level and share of total national income. Thus a generation ago someone in the topmost stratum of taxpayers—those who rank among the top 1 percent—earned about twelve and a half times what the median U.S. taxpayer made. But today a person at the top makes about thirty-six times (in real dollars) as much as his or her

10. Kevin Gunderson, an Occupy Wall Street protester, holds a sign at a New York City rally in 2011. Many Americans believe that government protects the rich at the expense of ordinary citizens.

median taxpayer counterpart. To be sure, in the same period wage earners at all other income levels have also secured some absolute real improvements in annual income. Yet the year-to-year changes at the very top have been much larger. The other ranges of income earners below the country's richest income earners have therefore necessarily experienced slowly declining shares of national income as more income inclined toward the top 10 percent, and even more for the top 1 percent.

Americans recognize the steady growth in income inequality, and many dislike it. Data from 2002 and 2004 surveys by the American National Election Studies show that a little more than 75 percent of Americans understand that income inequality has increased. Among those who perceived increasing income inequality, around 27 percent said that they had not thought about whether it was desirable. But about 44 percent perceived a growth in "the difference in incomes between rich people and poor people in the United States" and considered it "a bad thing." Just 4.7 percent perceived the increase and considered it "a good thing." More recent surveys with different wording show similar and widespread dissatisfaction with income inequality.

The American public, while famously optimistic about the economic rewards for individual effort and hard work, is now more willing to regard America as divided into "haves" and "have-nots." In 1984 about three-fifths of the public disagreed with the proposition that American society is split into these two groups, but by 2011 the figure had dropped to a little more than half of the public. Among the minority of 45 percent who agreed with the proposition when it was put to them in 2011, the majority were Democrats. Yet Democrats once took a happier view of American society. In the late 1980s only 32 percent of Democrats thought that America was divided into "haves" and "have-nots," but by 2011, 59 percent held that belief. Moreover, the percentage of Republicans who agree with this idea has grown noticeably, from 19 percent in 1988 to 27 percent in 2011.

Like climate change, the shift toward greater income inequality is far advanced and already shapes American politics, and this transformation cannot be easily halted or turned back. Income inequality—and its consequences for politics, culture, society, and the economy—will be there to analyze, criticize, or downplay for many years. The degree of income inequality that currently exists in the United States actually undoes all of the movement toward greater income equality of the 1930s and 1940s, and that lasted into the 1970s. Economists call that half-century of relative income equality the Great Compression. Today, though, the degree of income inequality in the United States matches that which existed on the eve of the Great Depression of the 1930s.

New facts about income inequality will continue to be widely reported. They are continuously available at, among other places, the website of the economist Emmanuel Saez, who in 2009 won the prestigious John Bates Clark medal of the American Economics Association in part for scholarship (in collaboration with the French economist Thomas Piketty), which persuasively documents the increase in income inequality.

Wealth and democracy

The new Gilded Age inevitably draws attention to the health of American democracy. An ancient problem in democratic politics is whether concentrated riches translate into concentrated power— thereby negating the premise of citizens' political equality. As the Nobel Prize–winning economist and liberal commentator Paul Krugman asks, "Why does this growing concentration of income and wealth in a few hands matter? . . . The larger answer . . . is that extreme concentration of income is incompatible with real democracy."

Krugman's problem boils down to two issues. The first is whether rich people can buy off politicians by paying for the costs of their election campaigns: campaigns cost a lot of money and they are not publicly funded. The second is whether rich people, or the lawyers and lobbyists who represent them, can show up at the White House or in the offices of members of Congress and demand special favors—for example, helpful changes in financial regulation or tax advantages.

Both campaign finance and government lobbying are to be sure elaborately regulated, but many citizens find the regulation of campaign finance and lobbying inadequate. The Supreme Court consistently opposes congressional plans for strong regulation of campaign finance. Congress, for its part, periodically enacts lobbying reforms, such as the Honest Leadership and Open Government Act of 2007—but one can wonder how much effect such laws have. Many members of Congress end their careers by becoming lobbyists themselves. This revolving door means that lobbying firms acquire the expertise and contacts that they need to make their case.

Campaign finance

For decades the Supreme Court has altered congressional efforts to limit the role of money in elections. The Court has insisted that campaign contributions and expenditures are a form of constitutionally protected speech. That point of view has gotten much stronger on the Court and is unlikely to change.

In January 2010, in *Citizens United v. Federal Election Commission*, the Supreme Court ruled that for-profit and nonprofit corporations, and trade unions as well, can directly spend money from their treasuries, without limit, on television, radio, or Internet campaign ads of any length—and in the process advocate the defeat or election of a political candidate. The Court held that the limitations on such advocacy expenditures that Congress enacted in 2002 violated the free speech protection of the Constitution's First Amendment. Corporations and unions cannot, however, formally coordinate their expenditures with any candidate.

Two months later, in *SpeechNow.org v. Federal Election Commission*, the U.S. Court of Appeals for the District of Columbia Circuit applied the *Citizens United* ruling to a case involving contributions (as opposed to the focus on expenditures in the *Citizens United* case). It held that any political action committee (PAC) could accept unlimited contributions from individuals.

Thus, by the middle of 2010 once defining aspects of campaign finance—upper bounds on both expenditures and contributions for independent political advocacy—had disappeared. Within the particular domain of independent political advocacy the principle of free speech now trumps the principle that previously inspired congressional regulation of campaign finance, namely that there is a public interest in preventing the appearance of corruption in electoral politics.

Ironically, though, the suspicion that money will in fact harm the political process was voiced immediately. When the Court handed down its decision in *Citizens United*, President Obama called it "a major victory for big oil, Wall Street banks, health insurance companies, and the other powerful interests that marshal their power every day in Washington to drown out the voices of everyday Americans."

A January 2012 survey picked up a related sentiment among the public. It found that about 18 percent of the public had heard "a lot" about a "2010 Supreme Court decision allowing unlimited independent expenditures on political ads," and about 36 percent had heard "a little." Of these two groups about 65 percent, in roughly equal proportions among Republicans, Democrats, and Independents, thought that the Court decision would have a "negative effect" on the 2012 presidential campaign. Such responses cannot be equated with President Obama's view that "the voices of ordinary Americans" would be drowned out after *Citizens United*, but they do suggest that the new campaign finance regime is not particularly popular with the public.

Critical commentary since *Citizens United* has noted that it is easy for fund-raisers and political operatives—and political candidates themselves—to evade the Court's caveat that independent political advocacy must be truly independent of campaign organizations. Informal coordination that meets the letter of the law but substantially contradicts the Court's requirement seems pervasive. Moreover, critics charge that it is easy for corporations and the super-rich to anonymously pass their contributions and spending through tax-exempt organizations that ostensibly promote social welfare via issue advertising. Critics point, too, to the 2012 presidential election, which witnessed a very significant increase relative to 2008 in billionaire and corporate donations to conservative and Republican-leaning issue advocacy organizations. Such revelations contribute to public unease with the new campaign finance regime.

What political scientists know about campaign finance

Political scientists are less certain that campaign finance ever decisively corrupts national politics. Both parties are highly competitive and quite good at raising money; both are staffed by competent campaign professionals and election lawyers who make sure that candidates comply with the law. The Federal Election Commission, established in 1974, and several nonprofit advocacy groups regularly release information about campaign finance, keeping the process fairly transparent and well reported in the media.

Although the absolute dollar amounts reported by the media may seem very large, they are actually relatively small. The scale of commercial advertising—for cars, toothpaste, pharmaceuticals, and other products—dwarfs the amount spent on election advertising. As a fraction of national income, the amount of money spent on national campaigns has risen only slightly over most of the past century. The great majority of wealthy individuals and corporations do not give money. Moreover, the super-rich—like the rest of the country—are themselves politically divided.

The parties also raise much of their national campaign money from a fairly small donor base that comprises about 10 percent of the ordinary public, somewhat more than 20 million people. They give at fairly low levels—between $100 and $200. A single donor can have disproportionate influence in sustaining a particular contender for a party nomination by spending on ads on behalf of that candidate via a so-called Super-PAC. But there is no instance of a Super-PAC sustaining the primary campaign that that party's own voters opposed.

The surge in harsh issue advertising that has resulted from *Citizens United* has certainly made elections more competitive. But it is not likely to manipulate voters in national elections. A malleable voter is someone who intends to vote, knows very little, has only weak partisan attachments, has not received any opposing views before election day—and is not turned off by strident attacks. The number of voters who meet that five-part description in a presidential, senatorial, or gubernatorial contest is vanishingly small. More voters meet that description in a congressional or state legislative race. The change in campaign finance brought about by *Citizens United* may affect some of these kinds of contests for a period of time. But studies of the evolution of campaign finance show that candidates and parties quickly learn how to remain competitive when the laws change.

What political scientists know about lobbying

Contacting members of Congress and their staffs is a constitutionally protected activity, and the details are publicly disclosed. When paid professionals do so it is unpopular—partly because of individual and well-publicized instances of bona fide corruption in Congress, which regularly recur. When President Obama denounced "powerful interests that marshal their influence every day in Washington," he seemed to have the facts on his side; after all, in 2009 about $3.5 billion went into lobbying Congress.

Real corruption, however, is the exception, not the rule. Members of Congress certainly contact bureaucrats and regulators on behalf of well-heeled people, but very seldom do they perform favors that they consciously consider bad public policy or harmful to their constituents. Political scientists have also never been able to find any consistent or strong relationship between lobbying expenditures and how members actually vote on legislation or in committee. Members of Congress typically accept money from organizations whose viewpoints they already agree with. The studies thus show that the two leading determinants of how members of Congress participate in the legislative process are their own perceptions of the interests of their constituents and their party affiliation.

Pundits often worry about unequal access to lawmakers. The provision by well-heeled lobbyists of slanted information—despite other strong influences, such as contact from congressional party leadership—would seem certain to sway members of Congress as they participate in making law and voting on the floor. Yet political scientists have shown that there are no policy questions in Washington that lack offsetting "sides" in that competing lobbyists and interest groups stake out positions in *all* major policy domains. Quite apart from the information regularly reported to it by the executive branch and regulatory agencies, Congress wades through seemingly unending waves of policy memoranda that promote rival points of view and rival solutions. The leading arguments about an issue are already known and much debated. In addition, members of Congress already have very strong policy views, which they acquire over the course of their careers in the process of taking stands during elections and studying the issues. Political scientists have never found that lobbying can turn a liberal Democrat into a conservative Republican or vice versa.

Representation over time

Political scientists of course recognize that particular groups are much better politically represented in Washington than others. Various kinds of industries and firms, such as large banks like J. P. Morgan, auto manufacturers like General Motors, or software manufacturers like Microsoft, are well represented by Washington lobbyists or have easy access to policy makers when they want it. Conversely, the poor and unorganized lack voices in the Washington conversation. There is, for example, no social movement or interest group that directly represents the unemployed. Starting and sustaining organizations that lobby on behalf of ordinary people and wage earners has always been very difficult.

Most ordinary citizens use their extra time for volunteering or religious observance, not politics. Very broad-based and participatory organizations with local chapters, such as the League of Women Voters or the National Association for the Advancement of Colored People, no longer attract new members as much as they once did.

On the other hand, political parties and elections engage and represent regular citizens. Americans may be economically unequal, but the party system tends to equalize them politically. The super-rich, divided as they are between the two parties, cannot control elections and their outcomes.

As the two parties have become equally competitive, the party system continually delivers opportunities for ideologically balanced representation. The mechanism that accomplishes such balance is the shift in public mood. The public's ideological mood will react to the current direction of government—creating a more favorable context for the political party that does not control the presidency. Republican presidents, by virtue of trying to push their preferred policies, produce a more liberal "mood" in the country—one that eventually affects national elections and helps Democrats. Conversely, Democratic presidents will generate a conservative "mood," which subsequently hurts Democrats and helps Republicans. In the end neither political party can rest easy. The relentless regularity of scheduled elections means that both parties must always expect voters to hold them accountable for what they do while they hold public office.

References

Chapter 1: Elements of American democracy

King quotation from *A Testament of Hope: The Essential Writings and Speeches of Martin Luther King Jr.*, ed. James Melvin Washington (New York: HarperCollins, 1991), 188.

Chapter 2: The presidency

On Woodrow Wilson, see Robert Alexander Kraig, *Woodrow Wilson and the Lost World of the Oratorical Statesman* (College Station: Texas A&M University Press, 2004) and especially Jeffrey K. Tulis, *The Rhetorical Presidency* (Princeton, NJ: Princeton University Press, 1988).

For the audience for FDR's fireside chats, see Betty Houchin Winfield, *FDR and the News Media* (Urbana: University of Illinois Press, 1990), 109, 121.

For the change in the percentage of American households with television, see Robert Putnam, "Tuning in, Tuning Out: The Strange Disappearance of Social Capital in America," *PS* (December 1995b): 664–83.

Time quotation: Michael Sherer, "White House Memo: Taming the Cyclone," *Time*, March 15, 2010, 18.

For the Brownlow quotation and details of his career, see Louis Brownlow, *A Passion for Anonymity: The Autobiography of Louis Brownlow—Second Half* (Chicago: University of Chicago Press, 1958), 298–99.

New York Times quotation on David Axelrod: Jeff Zeleny, "Obama's
Political Protector, Ever Close at Hand," *New York Times*, March 9,
2009.
For the Cantril quotation and details of his career, see Carroll J.
Glynn et al., "Public Opinion and Policymaking," in *Public
Opinion*, 2nd ed. (Boulder, CO: Westview-Perseus, 2004),
chapter co-authored by Carroll J. Glynn, Susan Herbst,
Lawrence R. Jacobs, Mark Lindeman, Garrett O'Keefe, and
Robert Y. Shapiro.

Chapter 3: Congress and its bicameralism

For the quotation from the *Federalist*, see *Federalist Papers No. 51*,
hosted by Yale Law School Lillian Goodman Law Library's Avalon
Project, accessed online at http://avalon.law.yale.edu/subject_
menus/fed.asp.
For the quotation from Obey, see Carl Hulse and Jeff Zeleny, "In Blow
to Democrats, Influential Congressman Will Retire After Four
Decades," *New York Times*, May 6, 2010.

Chapter 4: The legislative-executive process

For statistics on the history of the veto, see Kevin R. Kosar, "Regular
Vetoes and Pocket Vetoes: An Overview," Congressional
Research Service, November 18, 2010, http://www.senate.gov/
CRSReports/crs-publish.cfm?pid='0DP%2BP%2C_3%20P%
20%20%0A.
David Mayhew's findings are from Mayhew, *Divided We Govern: Party
Control, Lawmaking, and Investigations, 1946–2002*, 2nd ed.
(New Haven, CT: Yale University Press, 2005).
Nolan McCarty's findings are discussed in McCarty, "The Policy Effects
of Political Polarization," in *The Transformation of American
Politics: Activist Government and the Rise of Conservatism*,
ed. Paul Pierson and Theda Skocpol (Princeton, NJ: Princeton
University Press, 2007), 223–55.
Quotation from a former Senate parliamentarian on budget
reconciliation from Domenico Montanaro, "Biden Rules," First
Read, msnbc.com, March 1, 2010, http://firstread.msnbc.msn
.com/_news/2010/03/01/4425252-biden-rules?lite.

David R. Mayhew explains his estimate of presidential success rates in *Partisan Balance: Why Political Parties Don't Kill the U.S. Constitutional System* (Princeton, NJ: Princeton University Press, 2011), 58.

Chapter 5: The Supreme Court

Scalia quotation from Dahlia Lithwick, "Unprecedented," *Slate*, September 9, 2009.

Quotations from Supreme Court justices on being intimidated by the responsibility in Adam Liptak, "Heavy Workload of Complex Cases Awaits New Justice," *New York Times*, August 7, 2009.

Quotation from Elena Kagan, "Confirmation Messes, Old and New," *University of Chicago Law Review* 62 (Spring 1995): 941.

Rostow quotation from Eugene V. Rostow, "The Democratic Character of Judicial Review," *Harvard Law Review* 66 (December 1952): 208.

For public approval ratings of government agencies, see "Section 5: Views of Federal Departments and Agencies," *Distrust, Discontent, and Partisan Rancor: The People and Their Government*, Pew Research Center for the People and the Press, at http://www .people-press.org/2010/04/18/section-5-views-of-federal-departments-and-agencies/.

Quotation about oral dissents from Adam Liptak, "When Words on Paper Don't Convey Enough Ire," *New York Times*, March 9, 2010.

Chapter 6: Bureaucracy

Quotation from a public administration scholar from Paul C. Light, "The New True Size of Government," Robert F. Wagner Graduate School of Public Service, New York University, Organizational Performance Initiative, Research Brief no. 2, August 2006, 1, http://wagner.nyu.edu/performance/.

Quotation from Lisa Murkowski, *Sen. Murkowski Offers Disapproval Resolution to Block EPA Endangerment of Economy*, January 21, 2010, www.Murkowski.senate.gov.

Quotation from a congressional staffer on agencies' views of Congress from Jason A. MacDonald, "The U.S. Congress and the Institutional Design of Agencies," *Legislative Studies Quarterly* 32 (August 2007): 395–420, at 395.

Chapter 7: Public opinion and its influence

For statistics on voter confusion, see "Support for the Political System," *The ANES Guide to Public Opinion and Electoral Behavior*, University of Michigan Center for Political Studies, http://www .electionstudies.org/nesguide/gd-index.htm#5.

For the database of policy preference surveys, see Benjamin I. Page and Robert Y. Shapiro, *The Rational Public: Fifty Years of Americans' Policy Preferences* (Chicago: University of Chicago Press, 1992).

For more analysis of "numbered voices" and signals that voters send to politicians, see Susan Herbst, *Numbered Voices: How Opinion Polling Has Shaped American Politics* (Chicago: University of Chicago Press, 1993).

For the invention of the term "pollster," see Jean M. Converse, *Survey Research in the United States: Roots and Emergence 1890–1960* (Berkeley: University of California Press, 1987), 254.

Warren Rudman's remarks to Col. North are reported in "Iran-Contra Hearings: The Legislators Have Their Say—The Committee's Turn: Speeches to North," *New York Times*, July 14, 1987.

Rudman's remarks to a scholar on public opinion are from Amy Fried, *Muffled Echoes: Oliver North and the Politics of Public Opinion* (New York: Columbia University Press, 1997), 185.

For details on the *Literary Digest* poll fiasco, see David Karol, "Has Polling Enhanced Representation? Unearthing Evidence from the *Literary Digest* Polls," *Studies in American Political Development* 21 (May 2007): 16–29.

For George Gallup's discussion of Lord Bryce, see George Gallup, "Testing Public Opinion," *Public Opinion Quarterly* 2 (January 1938): 8–14 (Special Supplement: Public Opinion in a Democracy).

Chapter 8: Political parties and democratic choice

The text of Washington's Farewell Address is in Yale Law School Lillian Goodman Law Library's Avalon Project, http://avalon.law.yale .edu/18th_century/washing.asp.

The total popular vote in 1824 and 1824 is from David Leip, "United States Presidential Election Results," *Dave Leip's Atlas of US Presidential Elections*, www.uselectionatlas.org.

Whitman's poem, "If I Should Need to Name, O Western World," originally published October 26, 1884, in the *Philadelphia Press*, is in the Walt Whitman Archive, http://www.whitmanarchive.org/published/periodical/poems/per.00010.

David R. Mayhew explains median Electoral College "units" in *Partisan Balance: Why Political Parties Don't Kill the U.S. Constitutional System* (Princeton, NJ: Princeton University Press, 2011), 18.

Chapter 9: The partisan revival

For data on self-reported political ideology, see "Ideological Self-Identification," *The ANES Guide to Public Opinion and Electoral Behavior*, University of Michigan Center for Political Studies, http://www.electionstudies.org/nesguide/toptable/tab3_1.htm.

For survey data on self-reported voter turnout that exceeds actual turnout, see "Political Involvement and Participation in Politics," *The ANES Guide to Public Opinion and Electoral Behavior*, University of Michigan Center for Political Studies, at http://www.electionstudies.org/nesguide/gd-index.htm#6.

For national voter turnout and turnout by state, see Michael P. McDonald, "Voter Turnout," *United States Elections Project*, at http://elections.gmu.edu.

Quotation on a Senate candidate's campaign style from Michael Sokolove, "The 60th Democrat," *New York Times Magazine*, August 22, 2010, 24.

For data on political volunteerism, see "Political Involvement and Participation in Politics," *The ANES Guide to Public Opinion and Electoral Behavior*.

Chapter 10: Politics in the new Gilded Age

For the phrase "new Gilded Age," see Larry M. Bartels, *Unequal Democracy: The Political Economy of the New Gilded* Age (New York: Russell Sage Foundation and Princeton, NJ: Princeton University Press, 2008.)

The exchange between Matt Lauer of NBC and Mitt Romney is reported at http://thinkprogress.org/economy/2012/01/11/402671/romney-any-concern-for-income-inequality-is-about-envy/?mobile=nc.

For 2002 and 2004 data from the American National Election
Studies, see Bartels, *Unequal Democracy*, 144. For other survey
data, see Benjamin I. Page and Lawrence R. Jacobs, "No Class
War: Economic Inequality and the American Public," in *The
Unsustainable American State*, ed. Lawrence Jacobs and Desmond
King (New York: Oxford University Press, 2009), 135–66.

For views about "haves" and "have-nots," see "No Consensus About
Whether Nation Is Divided Into 'Haves' and 'Have-Nots,'" Pew
Research Center for the People and the Press, September 29, 2011,
http://www.people-press.org/2011/09/29/no-consensus-about-
whether-nation-is-divided-into-haves-and-have-nots/

Krugman quotation from Paul Krugman, "Oligarchy, American Style,"
New York Times, November 3, 2011, at http://www.nytimes.
com/2011/11/04/opinion/oligarchy-american-style.html.

Emmanuel Saez's website is http://elsa.berkeley.edu/~saez/.

Obama quote from Adam Liptak, "Justices, 5-4, Reject Corporate
Spending Limit," *New York Times*, January 21, 2010, available at
http://www.nytimes.com/2010/01/22/us/politics/22scotus.html?_
r=1&hp=&pagewanted=all.

For findings about campaign finance, see Stephen Ansolabehere, John
M. de Figueiredo, and James M. Snyder Jr., "Why Is There So
Little Money in U.S. Politics?" *Journal of Economic Perspectives* 17
(Winter 2003): 105–30.

For data on lobbying, see http://www.opensecrets.org/lobby/.

Further reading

Aldrich, John H. *Why Parties? A Second Look*. Chicago: University of Chicago Press, 2011

Bartels, Larry M. *Unequal Democracy: The Political Economy of the New Gilded Age*. Princeton, NJ, and New York: Princeton University Press/Russell Sage Foundation, 2008.

Baumgartner, Frank R., and Bryan D. Jones. *Agendas and Instability in American Politics*. 2nd ed. Chicago: University of Chicago Press, 2009.

Beltran, Cristina. *The Trouble with Unity: Latino Politics and the Creation of Identity*. New York: Oxford University Press, 2010.

Boyte, Harry C. *The Citizen Solution: How You Can Make a Difference*. St. Paul: Minnesota Historical Society Press, 2008.

Brewer, Mark D., and Jeffrey Stonecash. *Dynamics of American Political Parties*. New York: Cambridge University Press, 2009.

Campbell, Andrea Louise. *How Policies Make Citizens: Senior Political Activism and the American Welfare State*. Princeton, NJ: Princeton University Press, 2005.

Cohen, Marty, et al. *The Party Decides: Presidential Nominations Before and After Reform*. Chicago: University of Chicago Press, 2008.

Dawson, Michael C. *Not in Our Lifetimes: The Future of Black Politics*. Chicago: University of Chicago Press, 2011.

D'Emilio, John. *Sexual Politics, Sexual Communities: The Making of a Homosexual Minority in the United States, 1940–1970*. 2nd ed. Chicago: University of Chicago Press, 1998.

Derthick, Martha. *Keeping the Compound Republic: Essays on American Federalism*. Washington, DC: Brookings Institution Press, 2001.

Edwards III, George C. *The Strategic President: Persuasion and Opportunity in Presidential Leadership*. Princeton NJ: Princeton University Press, 2009.

Epstein, Lee, and Jack Knight. *The Choices Justices Make*. Washington, DC: CQ Press, 1997.

Erikson, Robert S., Michael MacKuen, and James Stimson. *The Macro Polity*. New York: Cambridge University Press, 2002.

Galvin, Daniel J. *Presidential Party Building: Dwight D. Eisenhower to George W. Bush*. Princeton, NJ: Princeton University Press, 2009.

Geer, John. *In Defense of Negativity: Attack Ads in Presidential Campaigns*. Chicago: University of Chicago Press, 2006.

Howard, Christopher. *The Welfare State Nobody Knows: Debunking Myths About U.S. Social Policy*. Princeton, NJ: Princeton University Press, 2007.

Katznelson, Ira. *When Affirmative Action Was White: An Untold History of Racial Inequality in Twentieth Century America*. New York: W. W. Norton, 2005.

Keck, Thomas. *The Most Activist Supreme Court in History: The Road to Modern Judicial Conservatism*. Chicago: University of Chicago Press, 2004.

Kettl, Donald F. *Leadership at the Fed*. New Haven, CT: Yale University Press, 1986.

King, Desmond S. *Making Americans: Immigration, Race, and the Origins of the Diverse Democracy*. Cambridge, MA: Harvard University Press, 2002.

Koger, Gregory. *Filibustering: A Political History of Obstruction in the House and Senate*. Chicago: University of Chicago Press, 2010.

Kriner, Douglas L. *After the Rubicon: Congress, Presidents, and the Politics of Waging War*. Chicago: University of Chicago Press, 2010.

La Raja, Raymond J. *Small Change: Money, Political Parties, and Campaign Finance Reform*. Ann Arbor: University of Michigan Press, 2008.

Lee, Frances. *Beyond Ideology: Politics, Principles, and Partisanship in the U.S. Senate*. Chicago: University of Chicago Press, 2009.

Levinson, Sanford. *Our Undemocratic Constitution: Where the Constitution Goes Wrong (And How We the People Can Correct It)*. New York: Oxford University Press, 2006.

Lien, Pei-te. *The Making of Asian America Through Political Participation*. Philadelphia: Temple University Press, 2001.

Mayhew, David R. *America's Congress: Actions in The Public Sphere, James Madison through Newt Gingrich*. New Haven, CT: Yale University Press, 2000.

McCarty, Nolan, Keith T. Poole, and Howard Rosenthal. *Polarized America: The Dance of Ideology and Unequal Riches*. Cambridge, MA: MIT Press, 2006.

Mettler, Suzanne. *The Submerged State: How Invisible Government Policies Undermine American Democracy*. Chicago: University of Chicago Press, 2011.

Mickey, Robert. *Paths Out of Dixie: The Democratization of Authoritarian Enclaves in America's Deep South*. Princeton, NJ: Princeton University Press, 2012.

Page, Benjamin I., and Robert Y. Shapiro. *The Rational Public: Fifty Years of Trends in Americans' Policy Preferences*. Chicago: University of Chicago Press, 1992.

Pierson, Paul, and Jacob S. Hacker. *Winner-Take-All Politics: How Washington Made the Rich Richer—and Turned Its Back on the Middle Class*. New York: Simon and Schuster, 2010.

Prior, Markus. *Post-Broadcast Democracy: How Media Choice Increases Inequality in Political Involvement and Polarizes Elections*. New York: Cambridge University Press, 2007.

Ramakrishnan, S. Karthick. *Democracy in Immigrant America: Changing Demographics and Political Participation*. Stanford, CA: Stanford University Press, 2005.

Robertson, David Brian. *The Constitution and America's Destiny*. New York: Cambridge University Press, 2005

Rosenberg, Gerald. *The Hollow Hope: Can Courts Bring About Social Change?* 2nd ed. Chicago: University of Chicago Press, 2008.

Schickler, Eric. *Disjointed Pluralism: Institutional Innovation and the Development of the U.S. Congress*. Princeton, NJ: Princeton University Press, 2001.

Shoch, James. *Trading Blows: Party Competition and U.S. Trade Policy in a Globalizing Era*. Chapel Hill: University of North Carolina Press, 2001.

Skocpol, Theda. *Diminished Democracy: From Membership to Management*. Norman: University of Oklahoma Press, 2004.

Skowronek, Stephen. *The Politics Presidents Make: Leadership from John Adams to Bill Clinton*. Cambridge, MA: Belknap Press of Harvard University Press, 1997.

Further reading

Smith, Rogers M. *Civic Ideals: Conflicting Visions of Citizenship in U.S. History*. New Haven, CT: Yale University Press, 1997.

Valelly, Richard M. *The Two Reconstructions: The Struggle for Black Enfranchisement*. Chicago: University of Chicago Press, 2004.

Vavreck, Lynn. *The Message Matters: The Economy and Presidential Campaigns*. Princeton, NJ: Princeton University Press, 2009.

Verba, Sidney, Kay Lehman Schlozman, and Henry E. Brady. *Voice and Equality: Civic Voluntarism in the United States*. Cambridge, MA: Harvard University Press, 1995.

Walker, Jack L. Jr. *Mobilizing Interest Groups in America: Patrons, Professions, and Social Movements*. Ann Arbor: University of Michigan Press, 1991

Wilson, James Q. *Bureaucracy: What Government Agencies Do and Why They Do It*. New York: Basic Books, 2000.

Wolbrecht, Christina. *The Politics of Women's Rights: Parties, Positions, and Change*. Princeton, NJ: Princeton University Press, 2000.

Yamin, Priscilla. *American Marriage: A Political Institution*. Philadelphia: University of Pennsylvania Press, 2012.

Zaller, John R. *The Nature and Origins of Mass Opinion*. New York: Cambridge University Press, 1992.

Websites

American political scientists now maintain several dozen excellent blogs; many of them feature constantly updated analyses of contemporary American politics and current public affairs. The most ambitious and influential is *The Monkey Cage* at http://themonkeycage.org. *The Monkey Cage* links to sites with American politics content, including *A Plain Blog About Politics* at http://plainblogaboutpolitics.blogspot.com, *Bessette-Pitney* at http://www.bessettepitney.net, *Matthew Glassman*, at http://www.mattglassman.com, *Mischiefs of Faction*, at http://mischiefsoffaction.blogspot.com, *Model Politics* at http://today.yougov.com/news/categories/model-politics, *Brendan Nyhan* at http://www.brendannyhan.com, *Presidential Power* at http://blogs.middlebury.edu/presidentialpower, *Rule 22* at http://rule22.wordpress.com, *Toward the Common Good* at http://towardthecommongood.com, and *Voteview.com* at http://voteview.com/blog.

Nate Silver of the *New York Times* produces largely statistical but still highly accessible treatments of national politics: http://fivethirtyeight.blogs.nytimes.com/author/nate-silver. The Miller Center of the University of Virginia places current events in historical perspective at http://millercenter.org/ridingthetiger. The American Enterprise Institute maintains a blog with freshly updated content about current U.S. public affairs on the front page of its site, http://www.aei.org. Two blogs about American politics that are maintained by Brookings Institution political scientists are those of Sarah Binder http://www.brookings.edu/experts/binders and William Galston http://www.brookings.edu/experts/galstonw. A self-consciously centrist think tank that offers political and policy analysis is *Third Way* at http://www.thirdway.org.

For the demographic foundations of American politics, see http://quickfacts.census.gov/qfd/states/00000.html, maintained by the U.S. Census Bureau, and the website maintained by a leading demographer, William Frey, at http://www.frey-demographer.org. For historical census data in an easy-to-use format, see the Historical Census Browser maintained by the University of Virginia libraries at http://mapserver.lib.virginia.edu. For polling analyses of Latino voters and blog posts about these analyses, see http://www.latinodecisions.com.

For the Constitution of the United States, consult the site maintained by the National Constitution Center at http://ratify.constitutioncenter.org/constitution/index_no_flash.php, and for the *Federalist Papers*, classic commentaries on the Constitution written by three of the Founders, Alexander Hamilton, John Jay, and James Madison, see http://thomas.loc.gov/home/histdox/fedpapers.html. For voting rights and citizenship over the course of American political development, see http://www1.cuny.edu/portal_ur/content/voting_cal, maintained by the City University of New York. An essential source for voter turnout and election administration is the United States Elections Project at http://elections.gmu.edu/index.html. To understand political issues in the United States and how they have been treated in the media and Congress, you can use trend analysis tools available at http://www.policyagendas.org. To understand ideological polarization in Congress, see http://voteview.com, which provides several reliable quantitative measures of ideology.

For the United States Code and for state constitutions, see http://www.law.cornell.edu/statutes.html. Other sites for understanding state and local governments are http://www.nga.org/cms/home.html, of the National Governors Association, http://www.ncsl.org, of the National Conference of State Legislatures. The Census Bureau lists and describes all local governments in the United States at http://www.census.gov/govs/cog.

For public papers, inaugural addresses, executive orders and memoranda, and other kinds of documents, browse the American Presidency Project, http://www.presidency.ucsb.edu, developed by two political scientists at the University of California–Santa Barbara,

Gerhard Peters and John Woolley. For a colorful interactive site on presidential history, see http://www.presidentialtimeline.org.

An excellent gateway to sites related to Congress is the National Archives and Records Administration's Center for Legislative Archives site at http://www.archives.gov/legislative/resources/internet.html. For the history of women in Congress, see http://womenincongress. house.gov, and for the history of African Americans in Congress, see http://baic.house.gov. For Latino members of Congress, see http://www.loc.gov/rr/hispanic/congress/contents.html. For LGBT elected officials, see outhistory.org/wiki/Out-and-Elected-in-the-USA:_1974–2004. The best source for congressional districting is maintained by Justin Levitt of Loyola Law School at http://redistricting.lls.edu.

For the Supreme Court and its history, see the website of the U.S. Supreme Court Historical Society http://www.supremecourthistory .org, and for more on the federal courts, consult the site of the Federal Judicial Center at http://www.fjc.gov/history/home.nsf. *Balkinization*, at http://balkin.blogspot.com, is a leading blog by law professors about the Supreme Court, public law, and judicial politics; it was founded by Jack Balkin of Yale Law School. Be sure to also browse http://www .scotusblog.com, an essential blog on the Court, the federal courts, the Justice Department, and the Solicitor General that is maintained by a legal research firm, Bloomberg Law.

The Louisiana State University Libraries maintains a site on federal agencies at http://www.lib.lsu.edu/gov/index.html, and for agencies that are now defunct, see the site maintained by the University of North Texas Libraries at http://govinfo.library.unt.edu/default.htm.

The essential source for public opinion is http://electionstudies. org/nesguide/nesguide.htm. Also enormously rich in its coverage of public opinion is the Pew Research Center for the People and the Press site at http://www.people-press.org. The subject index of the General Social Survey at http://www3.norc.org/GSS+Website/ Browse+GSS+Variables/Subject+Index offers additional coverage of American public opinion.

For commentary on the political economy from a liberal perspective, see http://www.epi.org/blog (of the Economic Policy Institute). Also quite valuable from a liberal and well-informed perspective is the *Scholars Strategy Network* at http://www.scholarsstrategynetwork. org. *Consider the Evidence*, maintained by the University of Arizona sociologist Lane Kenworthy at http://lanekenworthy.net, offers an incisive and even-handed discussion of income inequality and social policy issues. Somewhat more technical analyses of economic policy, tax policy, and the deficit are available at the Urban Institute at http:// www.urban.org/economy/index.cfm. For commentary on the size of government, regulation, and macroeconomic policy from a libertarian perspective, see the blog of the Cato Institute at http://www.cato-at-liberty.org. For the national budget, the Code of Federal Regulations, the Federal Register, economic indicators prepared by the President's Council of Economic Advisers, and congressional documents consult http://www.gpo.gov/fdsys.

To follow election law and campaign finance, the essential blog is Rick Hasen's http://electionlawblog.org. For commentary from a liberal perspective on campaign finance and election law, see the site of the Campaign Legal Center, at http://www.campaignlegalcenter.org and also http://www.gavelgrab.org maintained by Justice at Stake, and for commentary on the same issues from a conservative perspective, see the site of the Center for Competitive Politics at http://www .campaignfreedom.org.

For insight into group representation and policy advocacy in national politics, see Political Advocacy Groups, at http://pag.vancouver.wsu .edu and http://politicalactivitylaw.com, a website maintained by Eric Brown, a Washington lawyer who has served as counsel in several government agencies. Also see Open Secrets, at http://www.opensecrets .org/index.php, the Sunlight Foundation, http://sunlightfoundation .com, and http://votesmart.org/interest-groups, maintained by Project Vote Smart. For a sense of how persistent local popular protest evolves, browse http://bridgethegulfproject.com, which documents dissent in the Gulf Coast South in the wake of Hurricane Katrina and the 2010 BP oil spill. At the other end of the political spectrum, a conservative interest group that seeks to coordinate conservative policies among the states is the American Legislative Exchange Council, at http://www.alec .org. Think tanks play a vital role in American national policy debates; a comprehensive directory of them is maintained by the John F. Kennedy School of Government at Harvard at http://www.hks.harvard.edu/ library/research/guides/think-tanks-directory.htm.

Index

Page numbers written in italics denote illustrations.